DO MINERS READ DICKENS?

ORIGINS AND PROGRESS OF THE SOUTH WALES MINERS' LIBRARY 1973–2013

Hywel Francis and Siân Williams

Preface by Rhodri Morgan
Foreword by Dai Smith

Published by
Parthian
The Old Surgery
Napier Street
Cardigan
SA43 1ED
www.parthianbooks.com

First published in 2013
© Contributors
All Rights Reserved

ISBN 978-1-909844-44-5

Cover design and typesetting by Claire Houguez
Front cover image courtesy of Wales Council for Voluntary Action
Back cover image courtesy of South Wales Coalfield Collection, Swansea
University

Printed and bound by Gomer Press Ltd, Llandysul

British Library Cataloguing in Publication Data

A cataloguing record for this book is available from the British Library.

CONTENTS

MINERS' LIBRARY, SOUTH WALES

It is a memorial darkened
By the strafing of dust
And in the rooms shadows
Are full of stones over the dead.
Here I searched for my first books
In lean years of bibles
And tattered hopes.
Under the laden shelves
My appetite for meaning began –
The first pillar of a bridge
Between the mine's darkness
And the English Village
Of my present summer.

In these rooms miners,
Whose uncomfortable hands
Caressed worn volumes of escape
Into culture, were my tutors
Of toil and literature.
I have forgotten pages
From that apprenticeship
Though time has failed
To erase the memory of that
First discovery from the mysterious
Pattern of words which evoked
Ambition and the scorned image
Of the Exile's Trail.
That literary silence of the rooms

Still prevails. The ghosts
have multiplied and their miseries
Occasionally invade the conscience
Of a nation. Here, long ago,
Around polished tables, hungry eyes
Probed under scarred brows.
Men lunched on a book a day
And broken promises and nursed
A fading pride in jobless hours.
Dressed in blue serge they sang
Martyrs of the Arena
For a supper of prizes.

Their history is now a spiritual concession
Recorded in new books on the same shelves
That once bordered their besmirched lives.
The aged ones, who remain, recite
Their stories on park benches
At the feet of Prosperity.
The vanished men, memorialed in the mind
Are strangers to the new faces searching
For the same kind of magic
That is unchangeable and free.
It is easy now to blame these books
For my bridge that divides two loyalties.
I watch a youth take hold of a book,
"Take care," I whisper, "do not make a bridge."

Robert Morgan
28—1—83

Cynon Valley poet Robert Morgan presented a framed signed copy of this poem to the South Wales Miners' Library after giving a poetry reading there on 28 January 1983. Taken from *On the Banks of the Cynon*, Arc Publications, 1975.

PREFACE

Only one coal mine is now left in Wales, employing just 290 people. Barely credible really when there were 100,000 coal miners in the early 1960s and 250,000 at the peak a century ago. Most of us have coal mining in the blood. Both my wife Julie and I have coal miner grandfathers and have inherited the culture. That makes us pretty typical.

The South Wales Miners' Library started up in 1973, when coal was still Wales' biggest industry. It has survived and borne witness to forty years of decline almost to the point of disappearance, while dedicating itself to trying to understand how our post-coal, post-industrial society relates to that past.

I treasure my memory of taking part in an Energy Policy Seminar at the Library in 1988. Eighteen months after becoming the MP for Cardiff West, Neil Kinnock had just appointed me to be a junior frontbench Energy spokesperson. The Shadow Cabinet Member for Energy was a certain Tony Blair, of whom more was to be heard later.

The Seminar coincided with the start of the process of privatisation of the electricity industry. The Miners' Strike had finished three years earlier. We were in that post-strike closure period. Those taking part in the seminar were the NUM lodge secretaries of all the remaining pits in the Coalfield; some pits on the danger list, some apparently fine. The unmistakeable unruly straw mop of hair belonging to Tyrone O'Sullivan was visible at the back of the room. The other speakers were all energy policy heavyweights down from London.

To try to break down any possible Us and Them problem between the miners present and us VIP speakers, I introduced my lecture by explaining my 'loosehead prop' theory about why pits in Wales were put on the danger list for closure. To the total disbelief of the other speakers awaiting their turn, I explained that all loosehead props for Wales, in those far-off amateur days, were coalminers. Blaenant pit had been put on the danger list shortly after Llanelli's Anthony Buchanan, who worked there, got picked for Wales. However when the Welsh selectors dropped him and picked Pontypool's Staff Jones (Lady Windsor) instead, Blaenant got a reprieve. Unfortunately Lady Windsor went on to the danger list instead! The following season Cardiff's Jeff Whitefoot got the selectors' nod instead of Staff Jones. Whitefoot worked in Bedwas pit. Sadly, just as night follows day, Bedwas went on the danger list. My 'theory', such as it was, made everybody wake up.

Rarely have I enjoyed giving a lecture so much because here we all were, trying to work out where coal was going to fit in Britain's energy picture in the future. It was not Noah Ablett and William Mainwaring debating workers' control versus nationalisation. That was back in an era when no one could imagine a future where coal would become a marginal player in the energy world. It was real politics though for 1988. Welsh Coal was becoming marginalised. That's what the South Wales Miners' Library was facing up to, just as all those Lodge Secretaries were doing.

Recording and playing back that huge social and economic change in Wales has been a massive task for the Library. Its role has been crucial. I trust that all readers will enjoy this review of its forty year history.

Rt Hon Rhodri Morgan,
Chancellor, Swansea University

FOREWORD

'Knowledge is Power', proclaimed the banners they held aloft on their marches. To know would not only be to act; on the long march of coalfield society from the 1840s to the 1970s they had always known with righteous cause how to act. To know was to be enabled how to act effectively, and with intent to change the world. 'Where is Power?', asked Aneurin Bevan, and how, from Tredegar, could he get at it? Everywhere he chased it, he said, from Council Chamber to Parliament it disappeared around corners and evaded his grasp. He meant, of course, how could he fully operate the hidden levers of power in the wider society in the interest of the many who were excluded. He knew that he had been enabled to do so because he had already been given access to the power of knowledge. He had found it, and built it up for others, in that citadel of the intellect which was the Tredegar Workmen's Institute and Library. Nye Bevan caught up, tantalisingly briefly after 1945, with Power, and equipped with his knowledge from Tredegar he acted effectively and with long-term intent. The best parts of post Second World War Britain were the direct product of that vision of principle and pragmatism which the Institute Libraries of South Wales inculcated in their readers and supporters. In the true measure of these things it did not matter if not all miners read Dickens, or Marx or Morris or Ruskin, for enough of them did so to stand up for others, and those others understood that you did not need a diagrammatic rendering of their social DNA to feel what was common in inheritance and aspiration. Power is also what is emblematic of intent.

In the valleys of the South Wales coalfield, from east to west, nothing was a more literal representation of intent than the Institutes and Libraries. They were a three dimensional statement of purpose. They were a visual declaration of the secular redemption which this astonishing society was fast making its own. In township upon township, from valley bottom to side-stepping cwm, from the 1880s to the 1960s, they dominated the urban landscape of the coal gulches. They dwarfed all the public building that was previous to them. In truth, in these valleys built, as Idris Davies wrote, through 'the long Victorian night', their only rivals were square fronted stone chapels and the red-brick barracks of some public houses. The Institutes, inside and outside, were new and different. Even a century and more later, what is left standing, and what stays in the memory, requires the poetics of an architectural lexicon to begin to do them justice.

Pedimented doorways. Central mullioned windows. A sophisticated five bay composition. A four-storey classical composition which rises sensationally. Pale Doric pilasters. Dark ashlar ground storey. Red brick pilasters to carry a triglyph frieze across the facade. Segment-headed windows below and long round-headed ones for the piano nobile, with a bullseye window in the pedimental gable. The central doorway, a real showpiece, enriched with terracotta glazed, and unglazed, red, yellow and even blue. Faced with grey Pennant stone, two tall storeys over a basement. An intricate network of pilaster strips and stringcourses to frame round-headed windows. Fancy gable crowned with balls and asoteria. Grey rock-faced sandstone from Newbridge dressed with Ebbw Vale brick and buff-stamped terracotta panels. Two tall storeys. The skyline crowned on three sides by curvaceous pedimented gables. The entrance of three generous doorways, a central stone one with rusticated spandrels and swan-neck pediment. Polychromy of blue sandstone, red brick and white Portland stone. Finialed gable ends.

These pedimented palaces placed amongst us by community effort for communal need from the common treasure of wages, were no impediment to individual liberation. On the contrary, as the above roll-call of aesthetic embellishment proclaimed, from Aberaman Hall (1907–9) to Treorchy's Park and Dare Workmen's Hall (1913), from Nixon's Workmen's Institute and Library (1898–9) to Llanhilleth Colliery Workmen's Institute (1900), from Blaenavon's Workmen's Institute (1893–4) to Abercynon's Workmen's Hall (1904), and significantly from Maerdy to Glynneath and from Tredegar to Onllwyn, across the decades from the 1890s to the 1950s, such buildings sang out to the soul and met the changing needs of welfare, recreation and intellect from within communities which coalesced around their presence as the most enticing and vital part of their whole public life.

The exterior proclaimed power. The interior proffered knowledge. Inside, away from the commonality of the distended streets of terraced housing, or out of hearing of the metallic clangour of pithead wheels and the rasp of colliery hooters, the experience was one that was generally reserved elsewhere for only the metropolitan and the urbane. Here it was on the doorstep. It enticed. Throughout the 1940s and 1950s, to take just one instance, to step up from Cardiff Road onto the tiered front-steps of Aberaman Hall in the Cynon Valley was, in an instant, to cross over into a world of high-ceilinged calm and to walk on veined terrazzo floors. Along the walls, on display in their recessed niches, were white marble busts of champions of deed and thought, of Keir Hardie the constituency's and Wales' first socialist MP elected in 1900, and of writers and philosophers whose books could be found in the capacious library. Daily newspapers were laid out on high and wide wooden racks, above which plaques exhorted, in chiselled black lettering, teetotal behaviour, good manners and the shunning of gambling. There were downward slopes to be avoided as well as inspirational horizons to be sought. But this was no puritanical kill-joy environment. The basement once held a swimming pool. Balls clicked incessantly in the cool semi-dark of the four tabled billiard room, and upstairs the plush-seated theatre had been converted to a cinema. All was of a piece.

This is how John Newman in his magnificent volumes on Glamorgan and Gwent in *The Buildings of Wales* series steps back from his technical architectural descriptions of the Institutes to encompass their purpose. First, Nixon's Hall in Mountain Ash:

> 'Erected at the expense of the workmen of Nixon's Navigation Collieries, to provide for their mental and physical recreation. It provided on the one hand a library, reading and lecture rooms, and a theatre seating 1,500, and on the other billiards and other game rooms and a gymnasium, within the basement a swimming pool fifty-four feet long'.

And this on Blaenavon:

> 'A gargantuan affair ... expressing the self-confidence of the community in no uncertain terms... The interior contained an upper hall seating over 1,500 which could be used for theatricals. It was reached up a 'double grand stair', and on the ground floor were a newspaper room, a magazine room and a recreation room'.

The Institutes and their Libraries, monumental on purpose and multi-purposed in their culture, marked out the heyday of the working class civilisation which was South Wales. They permeated the novels of Gwyn Thomas from the Rhondda and the poetry of Idris Davies from Rhymney, they re-appear in the memory paintings of John Uzzell Edwards from Deri, and in the 1950s photographs of the American, W. Eugene Smith. Their centrality to our actions and thoughts has been testified to by the great politicians, Nye Bevan and Neil Kinnock, and by the miners' leaders Bill Paynter and Dai Francis. Most may now have crumbled or burned down or been left neglected, but the foundation of the South Wales Miners' Library in 1973 was proof of their continuing hold on our hearts and minds. It was an acknowledgment then, now forty years ago, that their values still validated us. That year was, significantly, sandwiched between twinned years of struggle and victory, between the national miners' strikes of 1972 and 1974. Now, in 2013, we must move on, often in and through the remaining and revitalised Institute buildings, to generate fresh Resources of Hope, in all those Valley communities, through the arts and in debate and by all those cultural activities which articulate the very meaning of our common humanity. And as we do so, to increasing intent and fresh purpose, the wisdom cradled and nurtured in the Miners' Institute Libraries will still speak to us, and guide our so necessary next steps.

Dai Smith,
Research Chair in Cultural History, Swansea University

NOTICE! WARNING!!

BAD LANGUAGE

IS
STRICTLY PROHIBITED
IN THIS INSTITUTE.

Offenders will be dealt with.

Phillips Bros., Printers, Aberaman

By Order of the Committee.

ABERAMAN WELFARE HALL

NOTICE!

Any Person or Persons found Damaging any Property of this Hall will be PROSECUTED.

By Order,
THE COMMITTEE.

PHILLIPS BROS., GENERAL PRINTERS, LEWIS STREET, ABERAMAN.

An Educational Citadel

Two Swansea University Professors in 1983 looked slightly bemused as they scanned the shelves of the South Wales Miners' Library. One said to the other, 'Do miners read Dickens?' We seek to answer that question, and a little more besides, in this special anniversary volume, which is also published to coincide with another Swansea University community initiative, the Science and Innovation Campus.

At the tenth anniversary of the South Wales Miners' Library in 1983, the distinguished miners' leader, Will Paynter, described the Library as 'an educational citadel'. He had always recognised that his own 'plebian' education owed much to the Cymmer Workmen's Library in the Rhondda: it was, as he put it somewhat sardonically and with a wry smile, 'his Eton'.

Our intention is threefold: to explain how this 'educational citadel' came about, to describe some of its unique holdings and finally to explain how it has, while remaining true to its historical roots, become a vital part of Swansea University's and the Welsh Government's current widening access and lifelong learning strategies within the communities of south west Wales.

We chronicle the origins of the Library, derived from the workmen's institutes across the South Wales valleys and their emergence as a unique educational and political phenomenon, 'the brains of the coalfield' as Dai Smith has called them. We will recall the remarkable partnership between the miners' union, the South Wales Area of the National Union of Mineworkers and Swansea University, supported by a major research grant from the Social Sciences Research Council (SSRC) between 1971–4. The remnants of the old libraries and other historical material were rescued by a team consisting of David Egan, Hywel Francis, Merfyn Jones and Alun Morgan, and shaped into this new Library, dedicated from the outset to research and new lifelong learning opportunities.

All this feverish salvaging activity was happening as the sharp decline in the coalfield temporarily ended, to be replaced by a rising tide of industrial militancy. All the British coalfields were once again the centre of media attention, even a history project of this kind. On New Year's Day 1973, the home news page of *The Times* led with a dramatic headline: 'Great working-class libraries of Wales destroyed by "ignorance, accident and plunder"'.

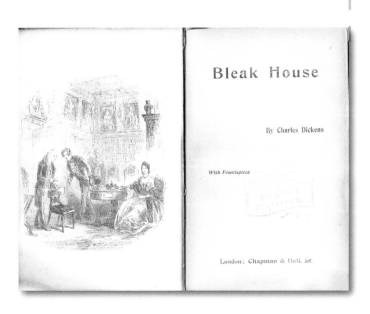

Left: One of the books by Dickens which could be found on the shelves of Miners' Institute Libraries.

HOME NEWS

Great working-class libraries of Wales destroyed by 'ignorance, accident and plunder'

From Trevor Fishlock
Cardiff, Dec 31

The great working-class libraries of Wales, some of them priceless, have all but vanished in the past 10 years. They have been bought up cheaply by dealers or lost or thrown away because their value was not recognized. There were more than 100 of them. Now, just in time, the last of the large libraries has been rescued as a dealer was offering £250 for it.

With the rescue, intact, of Bargoed miners' library and the remnants of others (a total of 11,000 books), a South Wales miners' library is being established at the university in Swansea to preserve what survives and to be a centre for private bequests.

Previously dealers had bought libraries for £40 or less. It is claimed that some books were sold in the United States for thousands of pounds.

The destruction of the miners' institutes' libraries of Wales through ignorance, neglect, accident and plunder is revealed in the report of a research team at University College, Swansea, working on a coalfield history. They began investigating the situation only last September, when they found that a dealer had bought two libraries for £20 each.

A combination of forces made the libraries in general vulnerable. With the rapid shrinking of the coal industry in the 1960s there were fewer miners and smaller grants. Library revenue and book stocks declined. As pits closed, the institutes followed suit in many cases and members were invited to help themselves to books, sometimes of considerable value. Other institutes became clubs and their libraries were sold to aid finances or were dumped to make way for cabaret and fruit machines. One club disposed of 5,000 books to make room for a billiards table.

A dealer paid £40 for one of the best and largest libraries in the Rhondda. With the advance of television and other social changes there was no longer a demand for the serious tomes in the institutes. Libraries were neglected and as many were lost in fires as were bought by dealers.

The university researchers put some blame for the libraries' disintegration on the negligence of public libraries and the "aggressive role played by opportunist book dealers".

The report states: "Several libraries have been sold off for small sums to book dealers who make quick profits on what were valuable assets in mining communities.

"The educational institutions in Wales have stood to one side and the destruction of so many valuable libraries is an indictment of them. County libraries, the National Museum and the National Library have ignored the problem and have often aggravated the situation by destroying collections through removing specialist or antiquarian volumes."

Miners' institute libraries have an important part in the social, educational and political history of Wales. They were financed by pennies from miners' pay packets and from 1920 were aided by a levy on coal owners. Nearly every mining town and village had its institute and library, answering the deep need for books and adult education.

The books were intellectual fuel for the growing Labour movement. Three generations of miners spent evenings after shifts educating themselves through the miners' institutes. Among them were leaders like Arthur Horner, A. J. Cook, Will Paynter, Noah Rees, Noah Ablett and W. H. Mainwaring. Tredegar Institute's library chairman in the 1920s was Aneurin Bevan and this library spent £300 a year on books, £60

being earmarked for philosophy works.

The best libraries were in the Rhondda and of the largest, at Clydach Vale, the university has saved 350 of 15,000 volumes.

Many libraries had outstanding collections of books on politics, economics, labour history, philosophy, psychology and religion.

Mr Hywel Francis, a senior researcher on the university coalfield project, said: "While many individual books and collections are valuable, the libraries have a greater value as complete entities. They are important as social and historical material and for what they tell us about the developing communities of the coalfield.

"By examining what they were reading we get an insight into the influences and aspirations of people in an area and an age where a whole working-class tradition was forged. The date stamps tell us about the popularity of key works and show clearly the decline of religious influence and the rise of left-wing politics.

"Of about 100 libraries, we have rescued one intact. Part of 17 others have been deposited with us. Thirty-three have been destroyed or have disappeared, mainly in the last 10 years. Others are not open to the public or have been incorporated into public libraries, and in many cases the books have been dispersed. Only three institute libraries survive in their own right and they are open only a few hours a week.

"We were lucky to get the Bargoed library. We raised enough money from sources in the university to outbid a dealer who had offered £250 for the 4,000 books, although one volume alone is worth £50. The institute committee could have got more but they acted responsibly and we hope others will follow their example."

The article that appeared in *The Times* on 1 January 1973. (Courtesy of *The Times*)

Its Welsh correspondent, Trevor Fishlock, described the cultural significance of what was at stake for the history of Wales:

'Nearly every mining town and village had its institute and library, answering the deep needs for books and adult education. The books were intellectual fuel for the growing Labour movement. Three generations of miners spent evenings after shifts re-educating themselves through miners' institutes...'

On 6 April 1973, Peter (now Lord) Hennessy quoted in the *Times Higher Education Supplement* Paul Johnson, the former editor of *The New Statesman*, 'these were the vehicles on which men like Aneurin Bevan built their political faith ... the intellectual source from which the workers would draw the means to build a better world...'

Hennessy also referred to the experiences of Fred Evans, the then Labour MP for Caerphilly, who had assisted in the rescue of the Bargoed Workmen's Institute Library. As a child he had benefitted from such libraries, having read most of Scott, Dickens and the Romantic poets by the time he was thirteen.

Preserving archives of Welsh culture and politics

Peter Hennessy describes the Coalfield History Project based at the University College of Swansea in Wales

A former editor of the *New Statesman* recently bemoaning the decline of working-class idealism took as the symbol of this collapse the sale or destruction of the miners' libraries in South Wales.

"A sickening tale of huge collections of books knocked down to dealers for pitiful sums in order to make way for cabarets and fruit-machines", was how he described it.

"These were the volumes", according to Paul Johnson, "on which men like Aneurin Bevan built their political faith. They were, in a real sense, pistols pointed at the entrails of capitalism, the intellectual source from which the workers would draw the means to build a better world—now swept away in a Gadarene rush towards meretricious pleasure."

Mr Johnson's elegy to a lost culture has, happily, proved to be premature. With help and encouragement from Dr Glanmor Williams, professor of history at the University College of Swansea and the South Wales Area of the National Union of Mineworkers, a team of young research workers at Swansea have managed over the past 18 months to save 17 institute libraries, amounting to over 12,000 volumes in all, from the bookdealers.

While researching a PhD on Welsh politics and the Spanish Civil War, Hywel Francis (son of Dai Francis, secretary of the South Wales Miners)

discovered that the material for his thesis, far from being available in the Public Record Office, was widely dispersed throughout the South Wales coalfield—in private collections of letters and papers and in the record books of the miners' lodges.

Out of this discovery grew the idea that a central archive of the cultural and political history of the region should be accumulated. An application was made to the Social Science Research Council who awarded £6,600 to finance three research workers and one secretary for a year. The Coalfield History Project, as it became known, was granted a further £23,000 to keep it afloat until July, 1974.

Swansea have provided the former library of their education department to house the collection and the South Wales Miners' Library will be officially opened in October to coincide with the seventy-fifth anniversary of the foundation of the South Wales Miners' Federation.

"We have now effectively put a stop to the dealings", said Hywel Francis.

"One of the dealers smeared us as 'romantic academics' for trying to preserve libraries no longer in use. We are romantics in the sense that we attach importance to the libraries as a part of the working-class heritage of the coalfield but we are also bringing them back into circulation for educational reason."

"It's a bit of testimony in itself", added his co-worker, Merfyn Jones.

The miners' libraries date back to the 1890s. With state provision of elementary education, miners devoted the money formerly spent on their children's education to the construction of workmen's institutes for their welfare and further education.

According to the project's first report: "In the two decades up to 1910, almost every large mining vil-

lage and town in the coalfield had begun building or had built its own institute, sometimes but not usually with the help of the coalowners."

Following the 1920 Mining Industry Act—which obliged the coalowners to levy one penny a ton on their output for miners' welfare—a further spurt of library construction occurred.

"Consequently, by the late 1930s there were probably over one hundred miners' institute libraries in the South Wales Coalfield. The biggest were in the Rhondda. Clydach Vale Library, supported by the Cambrian miners, is said to have had over 15,000 volumes."

With the contraction of the coal industry and the growth of alter-

native leisure activities after the war, the libraries went into decline, a process that became a rout in the 1960s.

The collections saved by the project vary in size from the 4,000 volumes of the Bargoed Working Men's Institute Library, which was acquired intact in January, to tiny individual libraries. Among these are the 150 book collection that used to belong to Jack Jones of Blaenclydach, a founder member of the British Communist Party and a veteran of the Spanish Civil War who was for many years a miners' agent in the Rhondda Valley.

In Hywel Francis' words: "His life is a history of the Communist Party in South Wales."

Tredegar Working Men's Library Foundation Committee, 1891.

The *Times Higher Education Supplement* article, 6 April 1973.
(Courtesy of the *Times Higher Education Supplement*)

COLLEGE TEAM DIG INTO MINE HISTORY

By David Blackwell

A SWANSEA University College team found they were only touching the tip of the iceberg — or perhaps the coal field — when they started research work a year ago into the last 100 years history of the South Wales coalfield.

The team's main intention now is to establish a South Wales Miners' Library in an independent building affiliated to the college, which will contain the wealth of material they have salvaged from the ever shrinking mining population.

But as well as collecting written documents and photographs, the team are collecting their history "live" — from the mouths of the very people who shaped the course of South Wales history.

Following a grant of £23,000 from the Social Science Research Council, the team of four have decided to use tape recorders for interviews with retired miners, union leaders, their wives and any other people who have memories of mining history.

"It is all very well to have written minutes of strikes and meetings," said Mr. David Egan, who is responsible for collecting material from an area roughly east of Swansea, "but the real history is in people's minds. The human side of things is missing. So much is contained in people's memories and reflections."

"Last year we were just contacting people and asking them for material, but now we are taping as we do our research. We are going back to others we know are good informants, and asking them for further interviews to be taped," he said.

At present Mr. Egan and his colleagues, Merfyn Jones, Alun Morgan and Hywel Francis, are each responsible for one area of the coalfield. But taping demands a fresh approach.

STUDIES

"We plan to make particular studies of small communities," said Mr. Egan. "Soon the whole team will go to Abercrave, which is a small mining community where the pit closed down in the early 60s. We want to talk to all the people, particularly the older ones, about the history of the community."

So far there are 14 master tapes lasting two hours each. All the recordings are transcribed, and the actual tapes will be put in a tape bank.

The research workers have the full backing of the National Union of Miners, and have collected minutes from many old Lodges. But some are irrevocably lost, especially in the pre-1945 period. Many records have been burnt, and others lost when officials threw them out as useless.

Other letters and photographs may not have come to light because their owners wish to hang on to them.

"Let me stress that we have full facilities for copying anything which must be returned," said Mr. Egan.

The project began in August last year when it was realised that much documentary material was in danger of loss or destruction as the coalfield contracts. An original grant from the Social Science Research Council financed a year's research, which unearthed masses of manuscript and printed material.

GRANT

The research had to continue, and a further grant of £23,000, given this year, will enable the work to run on for another two years.

"We have already given an exhibition at the Miners' Gala in Cardiff this July and at the Miners' Eisteddfod in Porthcawl," said Mr. Egan. "We showed many photos of documents and actual photos."

"As far as we are concerned, the older the material is the better. But we are not letting things slip, and we are keeping right up to date with newspaper reports of the last miners' strike," he said.

When the final collection is ready, it should be available to anyone wanting to do research into the history of the South Wales Coalfield.

The collection will even include whole libraries from Working Men's Institutes— interesting assortments of political and socialist works mingled with books in Welsh and other literature.

"When someone wants to know what a WMI library was like, we will be able to say here is one, exactly as it was," said Mr. Egan.

THE RESEARCH TEAM from University College, Swansea, with their tape recorder and some of the material they have collected in their comprehensive survey of the South Wales Coalfield. Left to right: Mrs. C. Jones, the secretary who transcribes the taped interviews and the team, David Egan (seated), Hywel Francis, Merfyn Jones and Alun Morgan.

A newspaper cutting about the Coalfield History Project which appeared in the *South Wales Evening Post* on 3 November 1972. It pictures the project team, L–R: Connie Jones, David Egan (seated), Hywel Francis, Merfyn Jones, and Alun Morgan. (Courtesy of the *South Wales Evening Post*)

Coalfield History Project Team members (L–R) David Egan, Merfyn Jones, and Hywel Francis pictured preparing an exhibition for the opening of the South Wales Miners' Library.
(Courtesy of the *South Wales Evening Post*)

L–R: Dai Francis, General Secretary of the South Wales NUM; Glyn Williams, President of the South Wales NUM; University President Lord Justice Edmund Davies; and Professor F. Llewellyn Jones, Principal of University College Swansea at the opening of the South Wales Miners' Library on 20 October 1973. (Courtesy of the *South Wales Evening Post*)

The holdings of the Library also include personal libraries of many who were prominent in the coalfield's history and large collections of banners, posters, paintings, maps, oral and video recordings, all of which were supplemented by a subsequent major research grant from the Economic and Social Science Research Council (ESRC) directed by Hywel Francis with Kim Howells as the senior research officer. These collections are complemented by the large coalfield archives, also rescued during the 1970s and 1980s, and now referred to as the Richard Burton Archives, following the acquisition of the papers of Richard Burton.

The educational trajectory of the Library was inextricably linked to the work of the University's Extra-Mural Department which appointed Hywel Francis as history lecturer and tutor–librarian of the Library. Initially the educational programmes related to local and labour history and day-release and residential course for miners. Following the demise of the coalfield in the years after the 1984–5 strike the Library's work took on a new direction. It became the Library of the Department and played a big part in developing the biggest community access programme in Wales from 1986 onwards and from 1993 delivering the biggest community-based part-time degree programme in Wales, initially through what became known as the Community University of the Valleys. The Banwen branch of the South Wales Miners' Library, in partnership with DOVE women's training workshop, became recognised across Europe as part of an example of best practice in widening participation to under-represented groups in higher education, particularly for working class women.

An advert which appeared in the *South Wales Evening Post* in October 1973. (Courtesy of Swansea University)

Kim Howells (right) was employed on the second Coalfield History Project from 1979–82. He filmed many of the interviews he conducted. (Courtesy of the South Wales Coalfield Collection, Swansea University)

Merfyn Jones interviewing John Evans of Fforestfach, Swansea in August 1973. One of the founding members of the South Wales Miners' Federation, Mr Evans died in 1990 at the age of 112.

Mrs Connie Jones, a Secretary employed on the first Coalfield History Project, transcribing oral history interviews. Over six hundred hours of interviews were recorded during that project.

We, the authors, have been intimately associated with the South Wales Miners' Library throughout its four decades. Hywel was the senior research officer principally responsible for the co-ordinating of the salvage operation and establishing the Library in 1972–4, as tutor–librarian from 1974–87, and then as Director of the Department from 1987 and Professor of Continuing Education from 1992 until 1999. Siân has been Librarian since 1995 and has overseen its dramatic growth in operation, supporting the educational programmes of what became known as the University's Department of Adult Continuing Education.

It is our intention to produce further specialist volumes of particular collections within the South Wales Miners' Library, notably the banners and the oral and video collections.

Top, left and right: Brochures advertising community and campus based courses offered by the Department of Adult Continuing Education.

Below: Graduates of the part-time degree programme in July 1998. They include the first cohort of Community University of the Valleys students. (Courtesy of Swansea University)

Archie Lush pictured with his lifelong friend Aneurin Bevan MP. (Courtesy of David Yendoll)

Opposite page: Tredegar Institute Committee, 1891.

BOOKS AND BRIDGES

'Well, where would you get these books?' This was the challenging and incredulous question of the Oxford tutor when interviewing Archie Lush, 'this sort of working class extra-mural student', as he described himself. It was 1927.

His confident reply still echoes down the decades, reminding us of the power of the written and spoken word, for Lush, for his friend Aneurin Bevan and for their generation of auto-didacts and worker intellectuals in the South Wales valleys:

> 'I said, 'Tredegar Workmen's Library'. Well, that convinced him I couldn't [have]... But I *had* read them *and* I was able to tell him what was in them!'

The South Wales Miners' Library was opened in Swansea on 20 October 1973 as part of the celebrations to mark the seventy-fifth anniversary of the founding of the South Wales Miners' Federation. In its first decade it was located in 'Maes yr Haf,' in a detached house owned by University College Swansea in the Uplands, a short distance from the main campus.

Yet the library's birth was an accident. It was the product of that unnecessary social and economic decline which enveloped the South Wales Valleys in the 1960s with the closure of ninety-one collieries between 1959 and 1971. In essence, it was the result of a salvage operation that attempted to save what remained of one of the most vital, dynamic and influential institutions in the South Wales coalfield, *the Miners' Institute and its Library*: the collective secular endeavour and achievement of the last generation of self-taught men and women in Wales.

It was this socio-economic crisis which precipitated the setting up of the Coalfield History Project in 1971 at University College Swansea with funds from the Social Science Research Council (SSRC), and, most important of all, with the full and active support of the South Wales Area of the National Union of Mineworkers. Two research students within the History Department at Swansea, Hywel Francis and Dai Smith, had become aware that, with the contraction of the coal industry, and the simultaneous break-up of traditional mining communities, invaluable records associated with the history of declining and disappearing coalfield institutions were in danger of destruction.

The South Wales Miners' Library contained the results of the Project's three years' work from 1971 to 1974. By the mid 1970s the book collection alone amounted to over twenty thousand volumes. Apart from the miners' institute libraries, there were personal libraries, notably those of the late S. O. Davies and Will Paynter, and also those of less prominent miners' leaders, over five thousand pamphlets, over five hundred hours of tape and video recordings, banners, photographs, posters, films, paintings, drawings, badges and maps. The manuscript material was lodged in the University Archives, recently re-named the Richard Burton Archives.

It is the institute libraries which formed the core of the whole collection, for they provided the original inspiration for the new South Wales Miners' Library and the spiritual signposts for its future. It was intended that the spirit and ideals of the old institutes would be recaptured in the new library and, it was hoped, would rekindle the burning desire for education: this was so much a part of the makeup of the Welsh miner in the early part of the twentieth century. The contribution of the miners' institute libraries in South Wales to the development of the Welsh and British society had, however, never been fully appreciated.

From the *Third Annual Report of the South Wales and Monmouthshire Council of Social Service 1936–7*. In the report Institute Libraries were described as 'the Public Libraries of the Valleys'. (Courtesy of Wales Council for Voluntary Action)

Brinley and Tillie Griffiths at their home, *Camden*, in Crynant. (Courtesy of Hywel Francis)

It should also be acknowledged that the personal library of the headteacher, Brinley Griffiths of Crynant, in the Dulais Valley, played a crucial role in the creation of the South Wales Miners' Library. A prominent member of the Independent Labour Party (ILP), adult education lecturer, activist in the cooperative movement and a conscientious objector in the First World War, he was closely allied to the leadership of the miners' union in South Wales. He and his wife Tillie, a Suffragist, had built up an impressive socialist library.

Their home, *Camden*, (so named after their favourite writer Walt Whitman of Camden, New Jersey) welcomed such illustrious visitors as James Maxton MP, Sylvia Pankhurst and C. L. R. James who may have completed his magnum opus *Black Jacobins* or possibly *World Revolution* in their home

so as to consult Brinley's library. Brinley bequeathed his library to the old South Wales Miners' Federation. This had been known to the union throughout the 1950s and 1960s and so there had always been the realisation that it needed a home. By the time he died in 1974 the Miners' Library had already been established.

One of Brinley's pupils was Menna Gallie, who based the headmaster in her novel *The Small Mine* on him. She wrote:

> 'The headmaster ... was a kindly, ageing Socialist whose gods were Marx and Lenin, with Tolstoi to make up the Trinity and D. H. Lawrence as a seraph in close attendance. He was as bald as a monk, with the face of a saint and patience to everlasting with kids'.

The significance of the miners' institute library is underlined by a telling quotation from the future founder of the National Health Service, the young Aneurin Bevan, whose generation owed much to the unrivalled reading facilities to be found in almost every mining community in the coalfield. At the opening of the first of two branch libraries of the Tredegar Institute in 1926, he placed his subject in its proper historical and social context:

> 'There is no colliery town in South Wales which could hold the candle to Tredegar for its library and institute; more money is spent on books here than in any institution of its size in Wales. But two institutions have grown up in the train of the industrialisation of the valleys which are more responsible for moulding the character of the miners than anything else and these were the Sunday Schools which cultivated the gift of expression and the Workmen's Institutes which [had] provided their reading facilities'.

In that same year, 66,715 volumes were issued from the Tredegar Institute Central Library. By 1947 this had risen to the all time record of 105,157 issues. By 1964 the Library, which had boasted 23,676 books a decade earlier, had been closed and the books dispersed. This was the magnitude of the crisis which confronted the Coalfield History Project in September 1972, when it embarked on the task of collecting what remained to form the one centralised South Wales Miners' Library.

Brinley Griffiths in his library in the 1950s. (Courtesy of Hywel Francis)

The earliest libraries in the coalfield really belong to the era of Mechanics' Institutes, Temperance Halls and Literary and Scientific Societies of the mid-nineteenth century. They were to be found on the south-western or north-eastern rim of the coalfield at such places as the tinplate towns of Pontarddulais, Gorseinon and Briton Ferry, and the old iron towns of Ebbw Vale, Tredegar and Rhymney. Many were absorbed into the proletarian institutions established largely by the miners themselves in the latter part of the century and the period up to the First World War; the Ebbw Vale Literary and Scientific Society weathered this change and survived under the same name.

Miners' contributions towards the building of their own institutes date from the 1880s and 1890s. It seems that the great explosion of institute building up to the 1914 war was primarily caused by the growth of the steam coalfield in the central valleys which experienced an enormous influx of population. The young men who came to such valleys as the Rhondda required institutes as an escape from the cramped atmosphere of their lodgings. Simultaneously, with the advent of free elementary school education, many miners appear to have diverted the pithead contributions they once made for their children's schooling towards the establishing and maintenance of workmen's institutes, thus providing facilities for their own further education. In the absence of universal state secondary education, and coinciding with an upsurge of interest in self-education, the institutes more than filled the yawning gap. Pressure also came from the general maturing of an *independent* 'labour' interest in education, politics and trade unionism throughout Britain at the turn of the century, with the advent of Ruskin College (1899), the Labour Representation Committee (1900) and, at a local level, the South Wales Miners' Federation (1898). The new lodges of the Federation desired a meeting place of their own, away from the alien influence of pubs and clubs, and the institutes provided the answer.

The library in Oakdale Institute.

In the two decades up to 1910, almost every large mining village and town in the coalfield had begun building or had built its own institute (sometimes, but not usually, with the help of the coalowners – the Tredegar Institute was generously endowed with donations from the local Iron and Coal Company). By contrast, the Bargoed Institute was completed in 1913 and the loan was repaid by 1921: the only support apparently received from the local coal combine, Powell Duffryn, was the permission given to deduct contributions from the miners' pay packets. Within each of these institutes a reading room and library was established and invariably these facilities became a focal point of the institute.

The libraries now being amassed appear at the outset to have had all the features of the philanthropic and craft institutions of the 1850s and 1860s, enveloped as they were in the ethics of utilitarianism, self-help and nonconformity. The Treharris Workmen's and Tradesmen's Library in East Glamorgan, which in its very name bridged the two traditions, contained 1,433 volumes. The juvenile section was dominated by the Religious Tract Society's List with such edifying titles as *Down in a Mine* or *Buried Alive*, *Alone in London*, *That Vulgar Girl*, *The Children of Madagascar*, *The Sunbeam of Factory Life*, *Servants and Service*. The shelves were crammed with *Chamber's Journal 1884–1889*, *Century Magazine*, *Hebrew Scripture*, *The History of Protestant Nonconformity*, *The History of Greece*, *Illustrated Abstainers*, Jules Verne, the lives of nineteenth-century notables, mining and mechanical works, Dickens, Henry Wood, Sir Walter Scott, Disraeli and works on Temperance (for instance, *We Girls*, *One Thousand Temperance Tracts*).

While a sophisticated Welsh readership is clearly discernible from the newspapers and periodicals supplied to the Library, there is only an occasional trace (notably with *Tarian y Gweithwyr* – The Workers' Shield) of an emerging political consciousness.

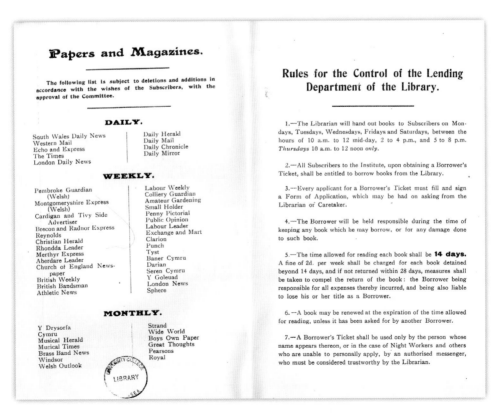

List of Papers and Magazines taken by Park and Dare Workmen's Library, Treorchy and its Library rules.

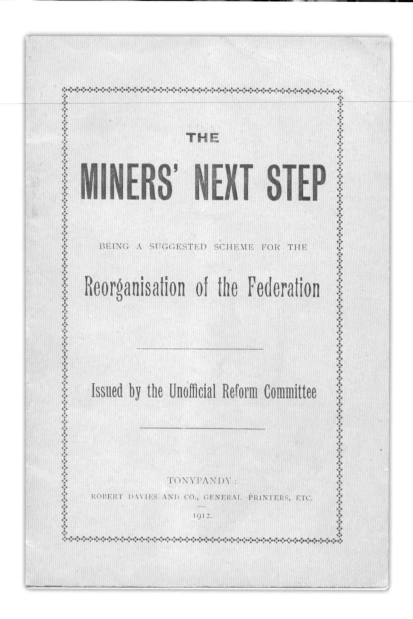

THE

MINERS' NEXT STEP

BEING A SUGGESTED SCHEME FOR THE

Reorganisation of the Federation

Issued by the Unofficial Reform Committee

TONYPANDY :
ROBERT DAVIES AND CO., GENERAL PRINTERS, ETC.

1912.

Cover of *The Miners' Next Step*, published in 1912. This rare first edition is one of many thousands of pamphlets at the South Wales Miners' Library.

By 1934, however, the Library, in reflecting the dramatic changes near and far, had moved, in the words of Thomas Jones, one time assistant-secretary to the Cabinet, 'from Palestine to Russia'. In a random selection from the 1934 catalogue, he chose the following 'strange authors and strange subjects':

Spengler, *Decline of the West*
Havelock Ellis, *Studies of the Psychology of Sex* (six volumes)
Bertrand Russell, *Marriage and Morals*
Bukharin, *Historical Materialism*

It seems that in the early days the control of book purchases was under the direct or indirect influence of the local colliery manager, the local nonconformist minister and other such benefactors. At Maindy and Eastern Institute (Ton Pentre) the large and apparently unused religious section reflected the interest of the local minister. At Park and Dare Institute, some books were donated by Rugby Public School.

The best example of a shift in power is at the Lady Windsor Institute at Ynysybwl where the miners wrestled control from the Ocean Colliery Company during the Great War.

With the notable exception of the mid-Rhondda, it appears that the institutes and their libraries did not become straightforward working class institutions in their content and activities until after the Great War. The historian can safely speculate that in the mid-Rhondda area, however, the large institutes and their libraries at Llwynypia, Clydach Vale (also with a branch library), Tonypandy, Ynyshir, Penygraig (the 'Dinas') and Porth (Lewis Merthyr) were already reflecting the advanced political, trade union and educational position embraced by the miners of the area. 'Speculate' is the only appropriate word to use: only 350 books have been saved from all these libraries which could in total have contained as many as forty thousand volumes. The Marxian Club, which was founded in Clydach Vale in 1904 and known locally as the 'Max', also contained a library, as did other workingmen's clubs in the area.

The local industrial turmoil of the Cambrian Combine Dispute and the Tonypandy Riots of 1910–11, the new syndicalist and socialist ideas expounded in the area by Big Bill Haywood of the Industrial Workers of the World or the Wobblies, Tom Mann and others and above all the momentous publication in 1912 of *The Miners' Next Step* by mid-Rhondda miners who had formed the Unofficial Reform Committee; all these developments were mirrored in the libraries. W. H. Mainwaring and Noah Rees, two of the authors of the pamphlet, exercised considerable influence over the Clydach Vale (Cambrian) Library as members of its book committee; Rees had also been a Ruskin College student in 1908, and Mainwaring was to become a lecturer at the new Central Labour College and MP for Rhondda East. The Cymmer Library, claimed by Arthur Horner and Will Paynter (two future general secretaries of the National Union of Mineworkers) to be the best in the Rhondda, boasted over seven thousand books in 1913: its Sociology and Political Economy section was beginning

to show signs of a Marxist intrusion, containing, among other titles, Aveling's *The Student's Marx*, the three volumes of *Capital* and Engels' *The Origin of the Family*. Wallace's *Land Nationalisation*, Proal's *Political Crime*, Nacquet's *Collectivism*, Henry George's *Progress and Poverty* and Belfort Bax's *Essays in Socialism* were other indications that the libraries were beginning to challenge Lib–Lab hegemony.

It was nevertheless not until the 1920s that the rest of the South Wales Coalfield began to catch up with the vanguard position of the mid-Rhondda area. The Great War, with the social forces unleashed in its train, was the catalyst which accelerated these pre-war trends.

As Bevan remarked in 1926, the miners' institute and the Sunday School were twin pillars of this unique coalfield society at the turn of the century. But with the end of the Great War, the institute was fast replacing and superseding the chapel, the vestry and the Sunday School. The roots, for instance, of the drama, of literature and of music in the coalfield had previously been in the chapel with its Gymanfa Ganu (Singing Festival) and Eisteddfodau, and in the vestry with its 'penny readings'. But with the emergence of financially sound institutes and welfare halls, such activities became increasingly secularised. In this respect, based on the whole community and reflecting the shared experience of pit life, the culture was strengthened against all manner of adversity – and such a secular revolution further hastened the demise of religion.

A painting of the young Arthur Horner. Painted in the 1920s by a visiting Soviet artist to Mardy 'Little Moscow'. (A bequest to the South Wales Miners' Library by the Horner family)

A Carnegie Trust Report in 1930 was perceptive enough to note this change:

> 'During the periods of unrest and unemployment, they [the Institutes] are the home of a large percentage of the male population, owing to the deplorable housing conditions. There was a time when church and chapel held sway in the valleys, but one of the legacies of the Great War is that the Federation and its officials and the Miners' Institutes took their place'.

The emergence of welfare halls as a result of the recommendations of the Sankey Royal Commission Report, which were embodied in the 1920 Coal Industry Act, did not in any way diminish this development. Although each Welfare committee had representatives of the coalowners and the public on its management committee and although coal companies were compelled to pay a levy for the upkeep of the welfare schemes, they tended to follow the same patterns as the institutes in asserting a more political role. The younger men who now came to the fore saw the institutes, welfare halls and their libraries as bastions to wrest from the grip of the coalowners.

But these were male domains from which women were largely excluded. The Quaker Settlements of the 1930s were much more enlightened, allowing women to borrow library books.

Each institute and its library mirrored very much these male-dominated communities. Some were more politically orientated and were seen more clearly as the property of the labour movement. For instance, during the 1926 lockout the Mardy Institute Committee released its fairly extensive assets for the purpose of paying half the cost of running a soup kitchen. Just to stand outside the Mardy Institute in the 1920s and 1930s was tantamount to declaring yourself a 'red'. Politics in such a community, which came to be known as 'Little Moscow' at this time, spilled over into every human activity – and all were centred on the Institute. But 'Little Moscow's' Institute Committee also tolerated a branch of the Young Britons and an Association of Unionist Women – an illustration, if nothing else, of the total political involvement of the community in the Institute. In such an intense atmosphere the Library quite naturally came to be seen as a revolutionary weapon to prepare the miners for the crisis of capitalism. Unfortunately we will never really know the precise content of the library – only one of its books has been located for the South Wales Miners' Library.

Other institutes reflected less demanding intellectual pursuits in the inter-war period. In spite of its fine library, Bargoed Institute was noted more for its boxing and snooker tables than its books. Every institute and its library was very much at the service of its community. However, the cultural, linguistic and geographical variations of the valley communities meant that each institute library had its own individuality and personality.

Will Paynter (left) on a 1936 Hunger March as it passed through Runnymeade. He was a regular lecturer at the South Wales Miners' Library in its first decade. (Courtesy of Harper Collins Publishers Ltd)

First right is Roman Roderiguez, killed serving in the International Brigades in Spain. Second right is the writer Lewis Jones. Will Paynter bequeathed his personal collection of books to the South Wales Miners' Library.

Will Paynter gives his own personal testimony to the political potency of institute libraries:

'...after the '26 strike, I had to go back to work nights, which meant I broke with my pals (they were working days), and I took to reading. Cymmer Library had... probably one of the best selections of literature that you'd find in any library in the Rhondda, and they were good libraries, the old miners' institute libraries in the Rhondda, you know: fiction, serious stuff, philosophy. I gradually gravitated to sociology. I sort of read myself through social

democratic [writers], Belfort Bax and that crowd, to Dietzgen, Marx, Engels ... there was no sort of design in the kind of reading, I suppose I read a lot more books than I had any need to, sort of wandering through it...'

All this coincided with a greater awareness of the publishing activities of the Kerr Publishing Company of Chicago which produced most of the Marxist texts for evening classes in the 1920s. The 1923 Catalogue for Cwmparc in the Rhondda contained among other works, volumes by Dietzgen, Marx, Trotsky (*Defence of Terrorism and Social* and *Industrial Reform*),

Untermann, Kautsky, Marx, Gide, E. and C. Paul, Haeckel, Thorold Rogers, Darwin, Vinogradoff, Ransome, R. P. Arnot (*The Politics of Oil*), Horrabin, Morel, Kropotkin, Lenin (*The Proletarian Revolution*), Fairchild and Thorstein Veblen (*The Vested Interests and Common Man*). The Gwaun-Cae-Gurwen Library revealed a similar pattern, although Jack London's fiction (fourteen volumes) and that of his wife, Charmian Kittredge London, (two volumes) seem to have been more popular there.

This whole phenomenon was fully appreciated by the Carnegie Trust Survey in 1929-30. It noted with some relief:

> '"Prolit-cult": It seemed at one time that the miner in South Wales was going to replace the old native culture with another – a culture based on his needs as a worker and fostered by means of the Classes organised by the National Council of Labour Colleges. This period has definitely passed and has gone the way of many other fashions in the political philosophy of the worker, such as the syndicalist fashion of 1910 to 1914. He is now groping back towards his old anchorages and is taking a new interest in music, in literature, in psychology, and in particular in religion, not necessarily the orthodox religion expressed in creeds, but in religion as expressing a philosophy of life'.

After the Depression and the Second World War, most of the institutes appear to blossom into a golden era. The outstanding miners' institute was at Tredegar, entering its heyday between 1945 and 1955. At this time it could truly claim to serve a community with one of the most mature proletarian and highly developed cultures in the whole of industrial Britain. What other public or working men's library in Britain serving a town of some twenty thousand souls could boast a Cabinet Minister (Aneurin Bevan) as one of its chief book selectors, a lending library of over twenty thousand books and a reading room which purchased the New York Herald Tribune and Pravda in 1946?

The Workmen's Institute at Tredegar became a most effective social institution in moulding the cultural and political tastes of the town for more than a generation. In the post-war era, £1000 was being spent every year on book purchases for the main library and its branches at North End and Troedrhiwgwair. There was also a comprehensive reference section, a

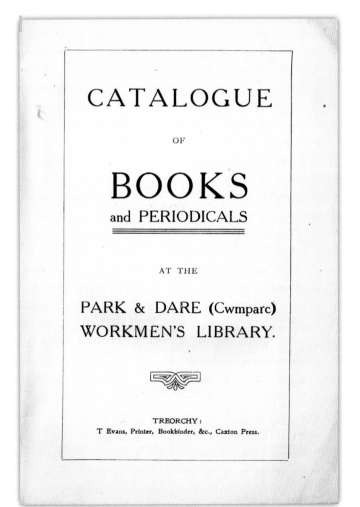

CATALOGUE

OF

BOOKS

and PERIODICALS

AT THE

PARK & DARE (Cwmparc)
WORKMEN'S LIBRARY.

TREORCHY:
T Evans, Printer, Bookbinder, &c., Caxton Press.

separate children's library (from 1957), a music library, a prints–picture library and a talking book machine. The Institute also supported a cinema, profits from which supported a film club and other seemingly minority cultural pursuits. By 1947 the Institute took financial responsibility for the Amateur Operatic Society, the Choral Society, the Orpheus Male Voice Party and the Town Band. It provided Library Scholarships for the children of its members in schools and universities as well as paying fees for music examinations. It sponsored its own music festivals as in 1948 when it spent over £1,000 on fees to bring international artistes to the town. The Institute's Gilchrist Lectures brought many eminent British intellectuals to Tredegar. These activities all thrived alongside the other traditional institute pursuits of snooker, billiards, draughts, chess, table-tennis and the cinema.

The significance of such institutes and libraries is thus self-evident. This phenomenon, on a *universal* scale, is peculiar to the South Wales coalfield: there was no comparable educational institution generated entirely by working communities anywhere else in Western Europe.

The ultimate demise of the libraries began in the late 1950s owing to a coincidence of factors. The provision of secondary education through the 1944 Education Act diminished the need, previously met by the libraries, for educational self-help. The local authorities, particularly in the Rhondda, began to establish their own library service and with greater resources at their command, would eventually undermine the institutes. The recreational revolution which overtook Britain – first television, then bingo, and lastly club life – had a devastating impact on the educational role of the institute. Finally, the real deathblow came with pit closures after 1959, when the pit-head contributions by the miners, which was the lifeblood of the institutes and the welfare halls, diminished to a trickle. Most of the hundred or so institute libraries which contained, according to one estimate, a total of 750,000 volumes in 1936, were decimated in the mid-1960s as a consequence of colliery closures and the growth of local authority public libraries.

When it was decided to found the South Wales Miners' Library in September 1972, it was widely, and falsely, believed that virtually all institute libraries had been dispersed. It soon became obvious that this was not the case and within three years major remnants of twenty-six libraries, and small sections from twenty-three others, had been salvaged.

Painting of Aneurin Bevan, founder of the National Health Service. (A bequest to the South Wales Miners' Library by Tredegar Workmen's Institute).

A similar, but somewhat less critical problem arose concerning the personal libraries of those South Wales miners who had emerged within the Labour Movement at the same time as the 'politicisation' of the institutes. The need for a 'home' for such books was no less important. Most of these miners, such as the future MPs George Daggar, S. O. Davies and D. J. Williams, had been involved in the independent working class education movement. Whilst the institute libraries were disappearing, there was a parallel loss of personal books and pamphlets, the extent of which is impossible to measure. Yet, for the historian, for posterity, and above all for their current and future use in working class education, they are indispensable. They give insights into the thinking of an influential group of local leaders – the worker intellectuals, checkweighers, co-operative activists, agents, political prisoners, stay-down strikers, rioters or International Brigaders – most of whom were inevitably National Council of Labour Colleges or Workers' Educational Association students and borrowers from institute libraries. But all of them quite naturally built up their own collections, and since this was a class which did not or could not amass personal manuscripts the contents of a man's library are crucially important for an understanding of his political and trade union outlook. The library of SWMF foundation member, Abel Morgan of Ynysybwl, with its concentration on the co-operative movement's authors, Brailsford, and Cole, contrasts with that of Max Goldberg of Aberdare, a CPGB foundation member. The type of education Goldberg received when being trained for cadre work at the Lenin School in Moscow between 1927 and 1929 gains a tangible presence in his textbooks, all of which are easily identified within his collection by the initials S. G. M. on each fly-leaf – Stanley George Morton being the false name given to him so as to protect his identity from possible agent-provocateurs within the Lenin School.

After the new Library was opened in 1973, it became a focal point for research into the South Wales Coalfield; three research fellows were based there. David Egan, a former member of the Project Team, undertook a survey of Welsh trade union and industrial records; Charles Parker, one of the pioneers in oral history, examined through tape-recordings the nature of class conflict in the South Wales coalfield; and Professor Helen Lewis, of the University of Virginia, undertook a comparative study of Appalachian and South Wales miners. Her work then and that of John Gaventa earlier has been sustained into the twenty-first century with educational links between the two regions.

From the outset, the Library became widely used by readers inside and outside the university. But, more importantly, it developed as a centre for adult and trade union education. In particular, day-release and residential courses were held for the younger members of the South Wales Area of the National Union of Mineworkers, whose grandfathers had made such sacrifices in founding the institutes in their localities. It was *their* heritage and they rightly saw the Library as theirs, especially during an era when there was a rekindling of the long and proud tradition in education amongst the South Wales miners, in the wake of the strike victories of 1972 and 1974.

"How to read Capital"

First. Read p.p. 364 – 378. From there, especially the four pages following, to the end of the section. It contains an application of the Mat. Concept. to Hist.

Secondly. Skip everything to conclusion of book, and observe how the plot turns out.

Thirdly. P.p 37 "Prim. Accum." is the biography of the capitalist.

Fourthly. Read P. 786 This chap. is one of the classics of Socialism; and with the chap. which precedes it, it constitutes an epitome of the philosophy of Socialism, that is P.774. Round these two chaps. have been waged the fiercest battles of Marxists and "revisionists". It is against the chap. on "Hist. Tendency" that Bernstein directed his heaviest batteries.

Fifthly. Read the first chapter, and proceed to the end of book, but must master this chap., and first nine chapters.

Notes from *Volume 1* of Karl Marx's *Capital* in the handwriting of George Daggar, SWMF student at the Central Labour College (1911–3) and Labour MP for Abertillery (1929–51). His library became part of the South Wales Miners' Library in July 1976.

The first NUM residential course at the South Wales Miners' Library in 1975. The guest speaker was Sir Archie Lush (front row, third from right). Among the tutors were co-authors of *The Fed* (1980), Hywel Francis and Dai Smith (back row, last two on right). Also in the photograph is Tyrone O'Sullivan (centre row, fourth from left), and Terry Thomas (front row, first left) who has been most consistent in his support of the Library and is still attending classes there in 2013. One of the set texts on the course was Dickens' *Hard Times*: these miners did indeed read Dickens!

On 24 January 1976, a plaque at the Library was unveiled by Will Paynter to commemorate the Welshmen killed fighting with the International Brigades during the Spanish Civil War. Subsequently, this attracted books, pamphlets, posters and other relevant material relating to that period.

It was considered then that Universities had a role to play during periods of socio-economic change, in creating such educational institutions as the Miners' Library and to do so through strategic regional partnerships. One of its supporters, Professor Glanmor Williams said at its opening, that the Library was a living testimony 'to the uniquely close and democratic association which has always existed between the University ... and the working men and women of Wales'.

Unveiling of Welsh International Brigades Memorial, 24 January 1976 by Will Paynter (first right). Also pictured are (L-R): Robert Steel, Principal of University College Swansea; Jim Brewer, Secretary of the International Brigades Association Wales; Dai Francis, General Secretary of the South Wales NUM. (Courtesy of the *South Wales Evening Post*)

Memorial programme for the unveiling of the plaque.

MEMORIAL

at the

SOUTH WALES MINERS' LIBRARY

(50 Sketty Road, Swansea)

to commemorate

The Welshmen who died serving with the International Brigades fighting Fascism in Spain

1936-1938

•

The unveiling of the plaque will be performed on Saturday, 24th January, 1976, by Mr. William Paynter, Political Commissar with the International Brigades and General Secretary of the National Union of Mineworkers, 1959-1968

THE MEMORIAL AND THE MINERS' LIBRARY

It is particularly appropriate that the national memorial to the Welshmen who died serving with the International Brigades should be housed at the South Wales Miners' Library : over half the Welshmen who fell in the Spanish War and over two-thirds of the 169 volunteers were from the mining valleys of South Wales. The South Wales Miners' Federation provided more for the Spanish Republic in men, money and materials than any other trade union organisation in the country. But the plaque, composed of Welsh coal, slate and steel, also symbolises the considerable support which came from other parts of Wales.

The simple bilingual dedication on the plaque represents the purpose of the memorial :

To the immortal memory of the Welshmen who with their comrades of Spain and of many nations in the ranks of the International Brigades gave their lives in support of the heroic struggle of the Spanish Republic against Fascism 1936-1939.

The memorial also contains in both Welsh and English, part of a poem by T. E. Nicholas entitled "In Remembrance of a Son of Wales who fell in Spain" :

He fell exalting brotherhood and right,
His bleeding visage scorched by fire and smoke.
E'en as the sweetest note is born of pain,
So shall the song of songs be born in Spain.

The Miners' Library has arranged an exhibition to coincide with the unveiling, depicting the Welsh involvement in the Spanish War. It is drawn from the growing and comprehensive collection already established at the Library and the College Archive. International Brigade volunteers, their relatives and friends and many of those involved in the Spanish Aid movement have deposited photographs, diaries, memoirs, tape-recordings, letters, Brigade newspapers, posters, books and pamphlets. It is intended that a room in the Library housing this material be dedicated to the memory of the Welshmen killed in Spain. The International Brigade Association (Cymru) and the University College are especially pleased that this should be established particularly as the Library was founded in 1973 to promote contemporary historical research and trade union and adult education. The Library will be glad to accept books, papers or any other material dedicated to the memory of the Welshmen who served with the International Brigades.

The Association wishes to thank all the sponsors and donors to the appeal without whose assistance this memorial could not have been possible.

Cymric Federation Press. Neville Street. Cardiff.

RICH SEAMS

For the past forty years, the South Wales Miners' Library has been a testimony to past generations of miners fervently committed to improving the standards of working class education. The collections assembled in that time richly illustrate that thirst for learning and self-improvement. They document the political, educational, social and cultural history of industrial South Wales in the nineteenth and twentieth centuries. The books, pamphlets, posters, paintings, banners and oral and video recordings have a common theme: the efforts of the men and women to enhance their lives, the lives of their children and the communities in which they lived. They are supplemented by the written records and the photograph collections held in the Richard Burton Archives at Swansea University.

Yet collections have not stood still. As collieries closed and communities changed, new material has been acquired. We can only give but a glimpse into the varied collections and reveal some of the 'jewels' held at the Library.

Friendly Society banner from Gwaun-Cae-Gurwen, the oldest banner in the South Wales Miners' Library's Collection.

The Naval Lodge banner was made in 1898, the same year as the founding of the South Wales Miners' Federation. For over fifty years, the banner had been kept at the Dinas Workmen's Institute in Penygraig. However, after the Colliery closed in 1957, the Institute building was sold to a boxing club and along with the Institute Library, the banner disappeared.

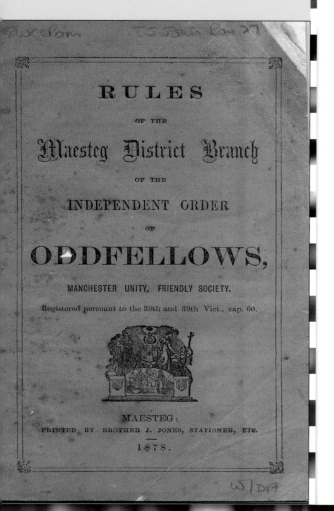

1898: The Welsh Annus Mirabilis

Seventy-five years after the founding of the South Wales Miners' Federation (SWMF), or the 'Fed' as it was usually referred to, some twenty union banners were proudly put on display to celebrate the opening of the South Wales Miners' Library on 20 October 1973. Located and collected as part of the Coalfield History Project, the slogans on these miners' lodge banners, such as 'An Injury to One is the Concern of All' (Wernos Lodge, Ammanford); 'From Obscurity to Respect' (Gelli Lodge, Rhondda) and 'Organise for Unity' (Mountain Lodge, Gorseinon) reflected the close involvement the union had in supporting the communities they served.

One banner which was not on display was from the Naval Lodge in Penygraig, Rhondda. This oil painted India rubber, pure silk banner is the only miners' banner known to have dated from 1898 and was made by the famous London banner makers, Tutill. Naval Colliery was in one of the most politically advanced areas of the coalfield of the time as its slogan, 'Labour is the Source of All Wealth', suggests.

The SWMF was the first coalfield wide union. Prior to 1898, there had been miners' unions, such as the Amalgamated Association of Miners which established itself in South Wales between 1870 and 1875. But such unions did not attract large followings. Instead, many miners were members of Friendly Societies, to which they would pay a weekly subscription in return for assistance if ill-health prevented them from working and a lump sum for the family when they died.

Left: *Rules of the Maesteg District Branch of the Independent Order of Oddfellows*, Manchester Unity Friendly Society, 1878.

Public Opinion.

DAME WALES: "Indeed, Mr. Employer, I am getting out of patience, look you. This wretched coal dispute might be settled at once if you would but join the men and arbitrate. I begin to think your cause must be a weak one, or you would not hold back !"

Staniforth cartoon from *Cartoons of the Welsh Coal Strike*, 1 April to 1 September 1898. This volume is part of the Library's extensive reference collection. J. M. Staniforth was the regular political cartoonist for the *Western Mail* from 1890. During the 1898 lockout, he produced a number of cartoons for the newspaper, which soon after the conflict, were published as a volume by the *Western Mail*. In the introduction to the volume, the cartoons are described as 'the production of the fertile brain and the facile pencil of Mr J. M. Staniforth' which 'will be found to constitute a Pictorial History of the longest and most disastrous dispute which ever afflicted the extensive coalfield of South Wales and Monmouthshire'.

Recalling the 1898 lockout, Abel Morgan of Ynysybwl, interviewed on 9 October 1972 said:

'Well I remember the ... 31 of March 1898, was the eve of the strike, and it was a beautiful night, moonlit night, and predicted a beautiful weather. And indeed from then until the end of August we had really beautiful weather and very often we had thunderstorms but ultimately we made the best of it. The first thing the lodge did then, they were not in any way organised only as a lodge committee, they then decided that they'd organise a soup kitchen in the vestry of the Noddfa Baptist Chapel. The Co-op contributed five pound per week during the whole of the period and the family received a jug of soup and a piece of bread according to the family and the children, but everybody had to go there and fetch it that wanted it ... And I enjoyed no work ... and I decided I'd travel the country walking the mountains. And I went to work on a farm ... haymaking, and I was reported to the lodge committee that I was working on the hay and my strike pay was cancelled'.

Defeated, the miners were forced back to work on 1 September 1898. The lack of organisation of the miners and the need for unity, prompted the creation of the 'Fed' in October 1898. This was a momentous political and social achievement: an Annus Mirabilis for Wales and the Welsh miners. Within the year, the 'Fed' had over 104,000 members out of a workforce of 132,682, as mining trade unionism took hold in South Wales.

Deiniolen (Caernarfon) Quarrymen as casual farm labourers. Courtesy of the late Bill Pritchard, this photograph appeared on the programme cover of 'Class and Community: The Welsh Experience', a Llafur/ Wales TUC/ Department of Extra-Mural Studies conference held at Swansea University in April 1979. The photograph dates from about 1900 and includes Bill Pritchard's grandfather (second adult on the left) who in about 1906, moved down to South Wales to work as a sinker in Glyncorrwg and Markham collieries before settling in New Tredegar. Bill Pritchard worked most of his adult life on the assembly line at Ford's (Swansea). He attended Ruskin College, Oxford before becoming a mature student at Swansea University. Bill was one of the speakers at the conference, and taught at the South Wales Miners' Library.

Dowlais, 1900. (Courtesy of the South Wales Coalfield Collection, Swansea University)

Migration into the coalfield also took hold with many travelling from other parts of Wales and the West Country in particular, in search of work. In 1901, 150,000 people worked in the industry in South Wales. By 1908, the number had risen to 201,000.

Dramatic migration into the expanding coalfield created a young and turbulent society.

One immigrant was J. L. Williams. Born in Merionethshire in 1888, he worked on farms before deciding to move to South Wales at the age of eighteen in 1906 to find work as a coal miner. His motivation was not simply to seek work but also learning opportunities:

> 'I had a desire to go for some years... my imagination I suppose had been fired more or less by some of the advantages of going to South Wales. I wanted to get away from the farms, and I thought there would be an opportunity for more self education in mining villages and that proved to be true'.

J. L. Williams describes how he travelled to South Wales:

> 'By train, the old railway. It was the Brecon and Merthyr chiefly joining it. Well the Cambrian took me to I believe Talyllyn Junction, and then the Brecon and Merthyr down to Merthyr. Oh I remember that journey very well. It was on a warm day in the month of May, and we were travelling through the Breconshire hills at a pretty slow pace I thought, and there was no signs, hour after hour past. The whole thing was very leisurely. The train stopped for a good quarter of an hour at one station with no explanation, until we found a lady coming across the field from a village with a basket of groceries and the train had been waiting for this young lady. And that was the kind of railway travel we had. And we got to Pontsticill, changing there the train was going on to Newport. I was going to Merthyr first. But there was still no sign of the industries we had heard so much about. We had heard about the iron works in Merthyr, to be seen before you'd see any coal mines, but anyhow, we came to a certain point, we started to go downhill and low and behold there was nothing but smoke in front of you for miles. There were the Ironworks, Cyfartha ... and Dowlais, and the pits from the Taff Valley down towards Merthyr Vale. So now of course I realised that I was in industrial South Wales'.

1910–1913: Militancy and Disaster

William Knipe, a Police Officer based in Pontypridd, and interviewed by the Coalfield Project in February 1973, described being on duty when the Tonypandy Riots broke out:

'We were called [to Tonypandy] on Saturday, November the 6th, 1910. And on the following Monday afternoon, that was the 8th of November, 1910, the redoubtable Will John, a Miners' Agent, held a mass meeting outside the Sherwood, Cambrian Colliery. And outside the entrance of this was a big embankment you see, full of stones, just nice lovely ammunition. Well anyhow, at this meeting, he declared that if they left the Glamorgan Police there, that they would see that there would be no disturbances, but if any foreign police was drafted in there, they would soon hold them out of it. Well the Chief Constable got to hear about this and naturally he straight away got police from Cardiff, Newport, Monmouthshire and some of the surrounding counties. And on Monday evening then they started rioting. And it was a ding dong battle for hours'.

As William Knipe also explained,

'[The miners] were fighting for what they ought to have had years before. Their wages were very low and I know for a fact they were working twelve hours a day underground ... they would be there half naked on their back and on their belly, hewing the coal out, for a mere pittance of a couple of pound a week. The only time they would see daylight was on a Saturday afternoon in the winter... [The Glamorgan police] all knew how they were living and how they were working and how honest they were.'

On 1 November 1910, twelve thousand miners employed by Cambrian Combine Collieries voted to go on strike to protest against low wages and the company's refusal to pay allowances for working in 'abnormal places'.

The tensions and frustrations in Tonypandy led to the Chief Constable of Glamorgan, Captain Lionel Lindsay, telegraphing the

COUNCIL MEETING,

PARK HALL, CARDIFF,

25th NOVEMBER, 1910.

PRESENT:

Mr. Wm. Abraham. M.P.. President.
Mr. Thos. Richards. M.P.. General Secretary.

Messrs. James Winstone. James Manning. George Barker. Edward Gill. Charles Edwards. William Vyce. John Davies. Walter Lewis. John Williams (Merthyr). C. B. Stanton. Enoch Morrell. Ben Davies. D. Watts Morgan. W. H. Morgan. T. George. Tom Harries. Thomas Lucas. Vernon Hartshorn. John Thomas. John Williams. M.P.. William Jenkins. J. D. Morgan. Daivd Morgan.

Also representatives from the Cambrian Combine Workmen's Committee. and representatives from the Aberdare Strike Committee.

Mr. Abraham explained the reason for calling this meeting, and asked the Committees if what had been reported to the Council was true. viz.:—

That a compact had been entered into between the two Committees that no resumption of work should take place by either of these bodies of Workmen until the disputes at the Combine Collieries and the Aberdare Collieries had been satisfactorily settled.

army for support on 7 November. The Home Secretary, Winston Churchill, intervened and the soldiers were held back. However, after more rioting and looting on 8 November, Churchill authorised the despatch of two hundred soldiers to Tonypandy; a decision which was to cause much debate and bitterness for many decades.

The lockout lasted for ten months, with the men returning to work defeated in September 1911. However, the issues of low pay and allowances for 'abnormal places' became a national struggle and resulted in the Coal Mines Minimum Wage Act in 1912.

The Cambrian lockout in mid-Rhondda had been the first major struggle for the minimum wage in Britain. Its ultimate achievement in 1912 throughout the coal industry was recognised universally as a significant trade union landmark.

Another legacy of the strike was the publication of *The Miners' Next Step* in 1912 by the Unofficial Reform Committee, which included Noah Ablett, W. H. Mainwaring, Will Hay and A. J. Cook. The pamphlet called for a minimum wage and a seven hour day. It also called for industrial democracy.

It was the beginning of notable changes for the South Wales Miners' Federation, as new radical leaders emerged, who demanded greater democracy within their union.

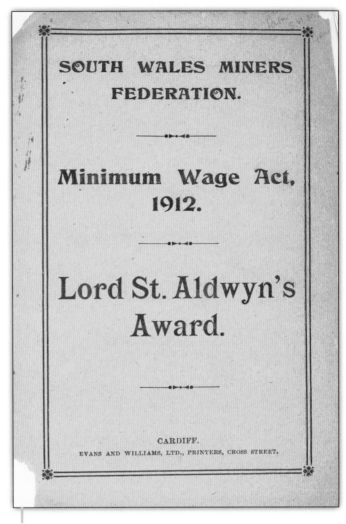

SWMF pamphlet explaining the 1912 Minimum Wage Act.

Left: Page from the SWMF minute book, 25 November 1910.

MARITIME COLLIERY Nº1 RESCUE SQUAD
SENGHENYDD EXPLOSION
OCTOBER, 1913.

S.W. RICHARDS   A. MULCUCK   H. DAVIES   J.H. THORN
CAPT.   (INSTRUCTOR)

W. WILLIAMS   L. PARKER

An explosion at 8.10am on Tuesday 13 October 1913 at the Universal Colliery, Senghenydd killed 440 people. It was the worst mining disaster in British history. Rescue teams from all over the coalfield came to assist, including Pontypridd's Maritime Colliery Number One Rescue Squad (above).

1914–1918: THE WAR AND THE COALFIELD

On 1 August 1914, the SWMF Executive Committee discussed at length a request from the Board of Admiralty,

> '...that those miners employed at Collieries supplying Admiralty Contracts should work on Tuesday and Wednesday next, two of the three days arranged as holidays by the Conciliation Board'.

The meeting rejected the request and proposed that an International Conference of Miners should be called in an effort to put pressure on Governments to avoid war. It was not to be, for on 4 August 1914, Britain declared war on Germany.

Tom Watkins of Ynysybwl, interviewed in October 1972, worked in one of the collieries supplying Admiralty contracts during the War. He remarked how hard the miners worked:

> 'There was nobody holding it back at all. They were all doing what the poor fellows in the trenches were doing, they were doing it down the trenches here do you see. And they were very loyal you know, fair play ... they had to work an extra hour to start with so that meant there was more coal coming out'.

Some miners wanted to enlist in the armed forces as an opportunity to get out of the pits, but others worked in the mines throughout the war, for there was high demand for steam coal to power the Navy's warships. William Rosser Jones of Maerdy, worked in the mines throughout the war. He recalls,

> 'I can remember going away, you were having leave then on the same basis more or less as the army ... and I

COUNCIL MEETING.

MINERS' OFFICE, CARDIFF,

3rd AUGUST, 1914.

PRESENT :

Mr. Jas. Winstone, J.P., Vice-President.
Mr. Alfred Onions, J.P., General Treasurer.
Mr. Thos. Richards, M.P., General Secretary.

Messrs. George Barker, E. Morrell, Thomas Lucas, Dd. Lewis, J. Williams, Noah Ablett, Tom Smith, Charles Edwards, Oliver Harris, Edward Gill, Dd. Morgan, W. L. Cook, Vernon Hartshorn, Hubert Jenkins, Wm. Vyce, Jas. Manning, J. D. Morgan, Wm. Jenkins, Albert Thomas, John Davies.

1.—Communication from First Lord of the Admiralty.

The Council was called specially to consider a communication from the First Lord of the Admiralty, upon the supply of coal to the Navy.

The following was a telegram received from the First Lord :— " T. Richards, M.P., Ninian Road, Cardiff.—In reply to your

Minutes of the SWMF Council Meeting held on 3 August 1914. At the meeting, the Council expressed 'its entire abhorrence against the War' but in order to 'secure a sufficient supply of coal to enable ample protection to be given to our food supplies and the protection of our shores', agreed to the Board of Admiralty's request and resolved to ask the affected miners to return to work the following day.

remember three of us going to Clevedon ... and in Clevedon at that particular time was a big hospital, full of wounded soldiers in their blue uniforms, and you felt uncomfortable see. But we were approached by some women who wanted to know why wasn't we in the army. We could do nothing else but show our exemption cards and that was in our favour all the time, that they had to have so many miners as well as soldiers see. So that exemption card was the key to covering you'.

As Dai Dan Evans explained, the propaganda encouraging young men to enlist was,

> '...from the pulpit, from everywhere. Inside the unions you see the Second International collapsed, so that politically and industrially, there was tremendous pressure. But as far as the coal owners were concerned, whilst they welcomed the lads coming back from the armed forces, they didn't want to see them go. They wanted them in the pits see'.

Will Arthur from Glynneath was one of the many miners recruited to join a tunnelling company:

> 'And this tunnelling company was going to be formed as a section of the army, to tunnel under the German trenches, and blow them up you see. Perhaps they would have to tunnel say, a 100 yards, 120, 130 yards see, and then blow them up... I walked in and joined. I was in France for a month, because they were not training the miners like, they were miners for a mining job see'.

Imprisoned Conscientious Objectors: Dartmoor branch of the Independent Labour Party, many of whom were from the South Wales Coalfield, September 1917. (Courtesy of Hywel Francis)

Not everyone was in favour of the war. D. J. Davies from Ystrad Rhondda was a Conscientious Objector. He was arrested in August 1918 and after appearing at a tribunal, sentenced to six months in prison, which he served in Wormwood Scrubs with other Conscientious Objectors including Arthur Horner and Mark Starr. D. J. Davies recalled being asked at the tribunal,

> '"What would you do if a German came and ravished your wife or sister?" Well I said I didn't have a wife which didn't help my case at all. "Well what if it was your sister then?" And that kind of nonsense, and "What if everybody behaved liked you, what would happen to the country?" to which I used to retort "If everybody behaved like me, there wouldn't be any war you see." But of course that kind of logic wasn't accepted inside of a tribunal ... really I was basing my objection on moral grounds then, not religious grounds...'

The war ended on 11 November 1918. As J. L. Williams recalled,

> 'After the end of the war, for two years there was still a big demand for coal and demand for miners, and then the big depression came and the coal trade like other trades caved in. We have never really fully recovered from that I don't suppose'.

Bust of Keir Hardie donated to the Miners' Library by Lance Rogers, the last Independent Labour Party councillor in Merthyr where Hardie, who had opposed the jingoism of war, was the MP from 1900 to 1915. The bust had been located in the old ILP offices in the town. (Courtesy of Hywel Francis)

Dai Dan Evans.

Dai Dan Evans was also a Conscientious Objector. He was a member of the Independent Labour Party and described how his decision was influenced by listening to speakers at meetings and by reading antiwar books and pamphlets, in particular,

'Brailsford's books were on the exposures of the war... And E. D. Morel's on the exposure of the war. But the books that affected me mostly on the standpoint now of developing a consciousness of, a working class consciousness, not only an antiwar consciousness, were the books of Upton Sinclair, Sinclair Lewis in America... Jack London's books, those were the books that developed my consciousness, my political consciousness'.

Below and right: Books that influenced Dai Dan Evans.

CAPITAL V. LABOUR.

TRUTH &

THE WAR
BY E·D·MOREL

1921: BLACK FRIDAY

In the years before the First World War, a number of unions had made efforts to forge links between themselves in order to coordinate united action. The Triple Alliance was formed in 1914, a coming together of the three most powerful industrial groups: the National Union of Railwaymen (NUR), the National Transport Workers Federation (NTWF) and the Miners' Federation of Great Britain (MFGB).

THE
MINERS' CONFLICT
WITH THE
MINEOWNERS

BY
JOHN THOMAS, B.A.
(*Miners' Agent, S.W.M.F.*)
Author of "THE ECONOMICS OF COAL"

With foreword by GEORGE BARKER, M.P.

INTERNATIONAL BOOKSHOPS, LIMITED
LONDON : 10 Johnson's Court, E.C.4
BRADFORD : 103 Kirkgate
MANCHESTER : 24-26 New Brown Street

The cover of the pamphlet *The Miners' Conflict with the Coalowners*, which was written in support of the miners. John Thomas gave a lecture in the South Wales Miners' Library in 1974, as the Coalfield Project was coming to an end.

The coal industry had been under Government control during the war. The Coal Industry Commission Act of 1919 recommended nationalistion.

The industry was making losses as the price of coal had fallen, and so the Coalowners demanded that the miners accept lower wages. The miners refused, and on 1 April 1921, a lockout of one million miners across Britain began. The miners appealed to the railwaymen and transport workers to come out on strike in solidarity, but on 15 April, or 'Black Friday', the leaders of the NUR and NTWF announced their members would not be taking any strike action. This caused much bitterness and saw the end of the Triple Alliance.

Max Goldberg from Aberaman, was working as a railwayman. Interviewed in 1972, he described how the miners organised themselves during the strike:

> 'Well during the strike of course they had all sorts of activities, for example in order to keep the miners together they ... used the Miners' Institute very much, in Aberaman you know. Of course we had quite a good Institute, we had billiard rooms and we had domino and draughts and chess rooms and we used to follow competitions to see if we could win something because if you could win a prize you used to get fags from it you see, or well the boys did. And they used to have competitions you know: singing and some step dancing ... the prizes used to be a parcel of groceries or things like that... And then of course they'd organize these gazoo bands and ... they had one in

Left: Painting of the Honourable Mr Justice Sankey. Sankey was a heroic figure because he recommended coal nationalisation and for that reason his portrait was hung in a place of honour in the South Wales Miners Federation offices in Cardiff, in the 1920s. (A bequest to the South Wales Miners' Library by the National Union of Mineworkers South Wales Area)

Below: The Coal Industry Commission Act, 1919, which set up the Sankey Commission.

practically every mining village in Wales ... they ... all had their own characteristics... some were dressed like convicts and some were dressed like prehistoric men ... and you would have forty or fifty bands competing ... they used to walk the mountains to come there because they didn't have fares.'

The lockout lasted for three months, until the end of June, when the miners returned to work, defeated.

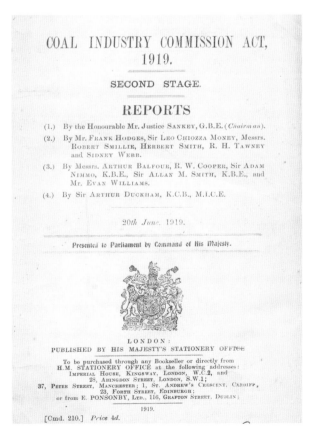

In 1976, the National Union of Mineworkers (South Wales Area) deposited Andrew Turner's dramatic portrayal of the 1921 lockout with the South Wales Miners' Library. The three panels depict solidarity, betrayal and defeat. In 2010, the Triptych was loaned to the National Coal Mining Museum of England for an exhibition of Andrew Turner's work entitled, *The Pits & the Pendulums – Coal Miners versus Free Markets.*

Photograph of the *Black Friday* Triptych by Andrew Turner.
(Courtesy of the National Coal Mining Museum for England)

D. DAVIS & SONS, Ltd.

FERNDALE COLLIERIES.

NOTICE!

The attention of all workmen is called to the fact that the output obtained from these Pits is so low that the question of continuing working is being seriously considered.

Unless the OUTPUT per man employed is IMMEDIATELY IMPROVED the Pits must stop.

1st November, 1921.

F. LLEWELLIN JACOB,
GENERAL MANAGER.

W. T. E. & Co., F.

'AND WE SHALL REMEMBER 1926...'

The Women's Page written by Elizabeth Andrews, which appeared in the SWMF's publication *The Colliery Workers' Magazine* in January 1926, expressed the deep anxieties of the women of the coalfield who did so much to sustain the home and the wider struggles.

Between 1898 and 1914, the coal industry continued to expand as new collieries were sunk all over South Wales. The production figures increased year on year to a peak of 57m tons in 1913. In 1914, Powell Duffryn Steam Coal Company suggested it had sufficient reserves to 'furnish an annual output of 4.5 million tons for one hundred years'.

However, after the Great War, competition from overseas coal exports saw the price of British coal and unemployment rise. In 1925, the Coal Owners asked the miners to accept cuts in the wages and to work an extra hour a day.

Right: *The Colliery Workers' Magazine*, January 1926.

Opposite: A notice placed at the collieries owned by D. Davis & Sons dated 1 November 1921.

20   THE COLLIERY WORKERS' MAGAZINE.

The Women's Page.
A HAPPY NEW YEAR.
BY ELIZABETH ANDREWS J.P., RHONDDA.

"Our young men are seeing visions.
Our old men are dreaming dreams.
And on mountain peaks already
Rising sun of wisdom gleams."
FRANCIS G. HANCHETT.

A Happy New Year to all. We have left 1925 behind us, and are facing 1926 with a clouded and troubled horizon. With problems that overwhelm us, we would despair but for **Faith and Vision.**

Labour hopes for the future, and urges us on to greater efforts and determination this year to try and remove the cause of all this misery and destitution.

In the mining industry we are almost hoping for some miracle to be performed in May. I hear many miners' wives say **we cannot hope much until May, then things may become better,** and the gleam of hope in their eyes when they say it show that they mean it. One marvels at the hope and patience of those who suffer so much. It is this **Hope** that keeps them from despair.

"The present system is based on the patience of the poor," is one of Dan Griffiths' sayings. How true this statement in the light of present-day affairs.

At a meeting the other day it was reported that there were little children in Blaina district, three years of age, who have never walked, and very little hopes of walking under the present conditions.

The children are suffeirng from rickets —a disease of **ill-nourishment and darkness,** which simply means lack of proper nourishing food, fresh air and sunshine.

Unemployment, with its attendants, **dissease and death,** have stalked through this district these last few years, and its effects will be felt by the next generation.

What is the remedy? The Prime Minister says, Less Wages, Work Harder, Longer Hours.

What does his Government promise us? More Taxes on Cutlery, Gas Mantles, Lace and Embroidery, Fabric Gloves, Packing and Wrapping Paper, under the guise of Safeguarding of Industries Bill; Unemployment —young men being scrapped off the Live Registers because their parents are working.

Economy in Education.

Circular 1371, issued recently by the Board of Education, suggesting a Block Grant System, has aroused all thinking people and progressive Local Authorities. It is the most reactionary document ever issued from the Board of Education. It has even shocked some of the Lords in the Second Chamber.

What does it mean? Instead of 50 per cent. of expenses on Education to be borne out of National Taxation, a block grant will be given to each Authority with a **do as you like sort of business.** If your Education costs more, the Local Authority will have to go, cap in hand, to the Board of Education to ask for more, like Oliver Twist. A refusal will mean an increase in the rates.

All children under five years of age are not to be admitted to schools, and 30 per cent. taken off the grant per child under

The Miners' Federation of Great Britain, under the leadership of A. J. Cook, fought against the proposal to cut wages and lengthen the working day hours using the slogan, 'Not a minute on the day. Not a penny off the pay'.

To counter this, a series of leaflets and pamphlets were published by the Coal Industry Publications claiming that miners' conditions had improved, their wages had risen and their output had declined.

A Royal Commission was set up and in 1926, it concluded that the coal industry was in need of reorganisation and the miners should accept a cut in wages. As an agreement between the coal owners and the miners could not be reached, on 1 May 1926, the miners were locked out and the coalfields came to a stop. The Trades Union Congress (TUC) supported the miners and called trade unionists to strike. The General Strike lasted for nine days between the 3 and 12 May. The TUC called off the strike, but the miners remained locked out until almost the end of the year.

Interviewed in June 1975, Merfyn Payne of Pencoed recalled,

> 'I think the women suffered most because they saw to it that the men had whatever there was going and the youngsters... I don't know a woman that would have pushed her husband ... not an inch to go back to work. I think they realised probably more than the men, because they the women had the continual struggle with bad wages, short time working, and the general running of a house. There was never enough money coming in for them to be at ease'.

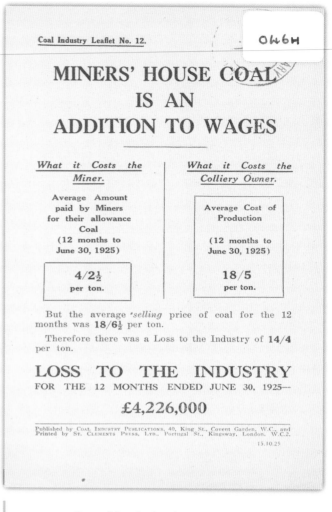

One of the Coal Industry leaflets.

Glyn Williams of Glyncorrwg explained that there was no unemployment benefit and single men were surviving on one meal a day from the soup kitchens:

> 'I've seen some fellows going around in 1926 ... looking for something to eat out of buckets ... although at the start of the strike it looked all right, fine to go, but as time goes on, you grind on month after month, it's hell of an experience'.

Above, and left: Some of the 1979 NUM Day Release class with the Gelli Lodge banner, which had been found on a tip and deposited at the South Wales Miners' Library. The banner dates from the 1920s and features the leader of the British Miners in 1926, A. J. Cook of the Rhondda.

Some miners spent their time during the lockout taking evening classes, such as those organised by the National Council of Labour Colleges (NCLC).

Others, such as the members of the Nine Mile Point Silver Band went on tour between May and November 1926, collecting money for their community. Elvet Evans of Cwmfelinfach described how they walked to London via the south coast of England, catching lifts when they could, playing on the street, in Church Halls or Labour Halls en route. The men collected well over £2000 to send back for the maintenance of soup kitchens.

Top: A Jazz Band certificate, 1926.

Bottom: A collecting box used during the Nine Mile Point Silver Band 1926 Tour. (A bequest to the South Wales Miners' Library from Elvet Evans)

The Band ended their tour by playing in the 'Great United Demonstration' concert at the Albert Hall in November 1926, organised by *Lansbury's Labour Weekly*.

Reg Fine of Maerdy described why and how the Character Bands and Jazz Bands were formed,

> '...more than anything, to take our minds off the real struggle you know. Well I myself was in the Character Band, what you call a Sheik Band you know ... they were all dressed up as Harem Ladies, veils on their faces and the beads...'

The Bands would march all over South Wales.

Will 'Post' Rees was a member of the Lower Cwmtwrch Co-op and in 1926, it had

> 'six thousand pounds of a debt ... and after the miners returned to work, practically all of them paid up what they owed... Well it took some of the big families over two years, but all the money came back, six thousand pounds.'

The Co-op played an important role in many people's lives in sustaining families.

Being a member of the Co-op enabled Mavis Llewellyn from Nantymoel to go to training college. She had been expecting to go Cardiff University, but as she explained,

> 'I was the eldest of three, and it was twenty-six and they were out. Although the strike was over, our family had been victimised. Dad couldn't get work, Fred wasn't working, so there was nothing for it. I had to go to college for two years. And then, the only way in which college fees could be paid was co-op dividend. We had always been co-operators, and the last of the dividend was drawn out to pay my last fees. Because we had to pay our own fees then, there were no grants. And I went on co-op dividend'.

International Class War Prisoners Aid (ICWPA) certificate presented to Oliver James of Seven Sisters after he served a prison sentence because of his role in the Anthracite Strike.

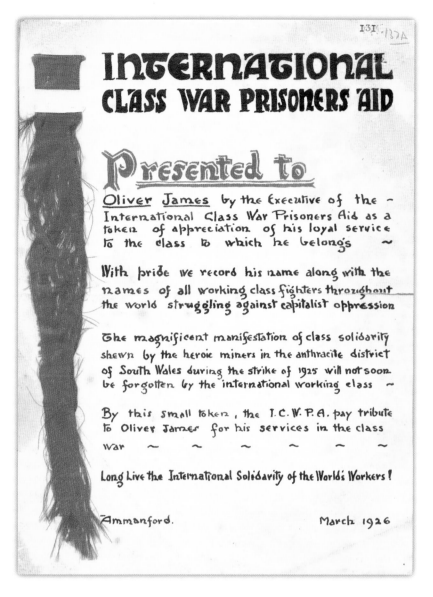

Many women at this time worked in domestic service. Maria Williams of Maerdy noted when interviewed in July 1973, 'all my friends had gone away. They were all going away to service you see'. Maria described how at the age of seventeen her mother took her to Pontypridd where she was accepted on a domestic training course.

> '...it was a three month course and it was excellent because I mean they taught us sewing, when we did our own uniforms, morning uniforms and afternoon. And then we did all the housework, all the house duties. We were living in a big house at the time and it was exactly as if you were in private service'.

At the end of the course, Maria was found employment in London. She worked for a number of families there before returning to Maerdy in 1936.

The 1926 lockout ended in total defeat, followed by long years of unemployment and the steep decline in the power of the Fed. Many miners, following confrontations with the police, were imprisoned in 1926. Tommy Nicholas who worked in the Dulais Valley received a medal from the International Class War Prisoners Aid (ICWPA) following his release from prison. Sam Morris of Ammanford was another recipient of a medal. Earlier in the year, Oliver James of Seven Sisters (veteran of the 1925 Anthracite struggle) received an ICWPA certificate.

South Wales Marchers' Organising Council.

SOUTH WALES MINERS'
MARCH TO LONDON

CALL TO ACTION! VOLUNTEERS WANTED!

Arising out of the pronouncement by A. J. COOK, 18/9/27, a Miners' March to London from S. Wales is being organised. The March will commence on the day Parliament opens--Nov. 8th, and the Marchers will arrive in London on Nov. 20th, where they will be received by an <u>All London</u> Working Class Demonstration.

The object of the March shall be two-fold, to arouse a Nation-wide feeling concerning the Appalling Conditions in the Minefields created by the policy of the Government and the Coal-owners, and to seek an interview with the Prime Minister, the Minister of Mines, the Minister of Labour, and the Minister of Health.

The purpose of such interview shall be :

1. To draw attention to the Chronic Destitution affecting Unemployed and Employed Miners arising out of the Failure of Private Enterprise in the Mining Industry.

2. To draw the attention of the Government to the persistent Closing of Mines, thus causing further widespread Unemployment.

3. To point out the consequences of the 8-hour Day.

4. To urge the Government to make Satisfactory Provision for the Employment of those Unemployed.

5. To demand State Aid to permit Guardians to more effectively Relieve Distress.

6. To protest against the Continuous Disqualification of Men and Women from Benefit at the Labour Exchange, and to urge More Adequate Scales of Benefit.

7. To press for a system of Adequate Pensioning of Miners over Sixty Years of age as a means of Reducing the Number of Unemployed.

☛ Those wishing to Enrol as Recruits for this Historic March should make application at once to :

THE TRAGEDY OF THE MINEFIELDS MUST BE MADE KNOWN !

Thomas Bros., Printers, &c., Pandy Square, Tonypendy

POVERTY, DOLE AND ANTI-FASCISM IN THE 1930S

The 1930s brought unemployment, poverty, disease and despair to the South Wales coalfield. By 1931, 140,000 miners were out of work.

The National Unemployed Workers' Movement was established, and working with the SWMF, organised a number of Hunger Marches in the late 1920s and 1930s. Demonstrations against the Means Test in 1935 were also held to draw attention to the desperate plight in which the unemployed miners and their families found themselves.

The Hunger Marches which left South Wales between 1927 and 1936 to protest against worsening conditions in the coal industry produced a number of banners. So concerned were the police with the marchers that the slogans on the banners were often reported.

During one of the Hunger Marches, a group of miners were singing as they walked along a street in London in an effort to raise money for food. A chance meeting with the American singer, actor and civil rights activist, Paul Robeson, who was appearing in the stage production of *Show Boat* on Drury Lane, saw the miners forge a close friendship with Paul Robeson, which lasted until he died in 1976. Robeson felt a strong affinity with Wales and its culture built around the values of community and work. He visited Wales several times. On 7 December 1938, Paul attended the Welsh National Memorial Meeting in Mountain Ash, which had been organised to commemorate the thirty three men from Wales who had not returned from Spain after volunteering to fight in the Spanish Civil War.

Right: Portrait of Paul Robeson by Armenian–Canadian photographer Yousuf Karsh. (Courtesy the Estate of Yousuf Karsh)

Opposite: Poster calling for support for the first Hunger March from South Wales in 1927.

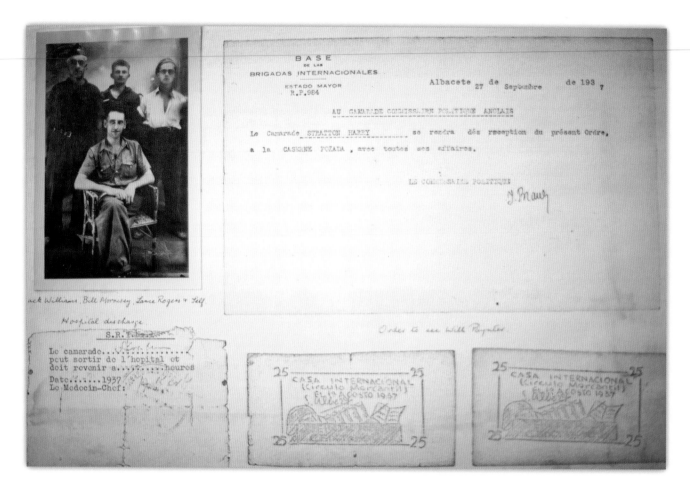

Extract from Harry Stratton's Spanish scrapbook. Harry Stratton, a taxi driver from Swansea, joined the International Brigades in 1937. Harry Stratton's son, Les, presented his father's scrapbook to the South Wales Miners' Library during an event to launch the new edition of the book, *Miners Against Fascism* by Hywel Francis, on 30 June 2012.

In response to the rise of fascism in Europe and the outbreak of the Spanish Civil War in July 1936, 134 men from South Wales volunteered to join the International Brigades and support the Republican cause. Jim Brewer, from Rhymney, went out to Spain in 1937:

> 'We booked for Paris and they warned us not to go as a bunch but walk around as individuals ... as though you were part of a crowd you see. Well it was hell of a difficult thing to do, and some of our blokes weren't very bright at doing it, and so I stood aside now and let them all take their tickets and

got mine last of all. I whipped smartly around the kiosk and there was a man with big feet there who put his nose into the clerk and asked "Where did those chaps book for?" So the clerk told him ... and he'd shown his warrant see, so we kept an eye on this bloke now. He followed us all the way to Paris... Then we were off to this place Arles in the south of France ... and we moved into the old town hall ... there must have been about four hundred of us there... If the municipality of Arles didn't know we were there, well they must have had thick blinkers on... Then we had to move out, all secret journey now you know, another taxi down near the border... Well this route took us past a farmhouse and we had to go round two sides of it ... and we were going about nine o'clock at night I think, about twenty of us in single file, and this dog barking his head off and nobody came out to look... Well then we had to cross an international bridge somewhere and they said "Be very careful going across here, keep on your hands and knees. Go silently and don't make a noise..." Now all we were supposed to take was a change of underwear and socks and a razor blade... Well I had my gillette now disposed around my waistcoat pockets and ... when I got to the centre of this bridge ... the handle of this gillette razor blade fell out and that went clonk, clonk, clonk, on the steel girders ... and you can imagine, it was like a bullet at that time of night. And then the other bits fell out and the whole operation was given away, if there'd been anybody listening.'

In many areas, meetings, rallies and food collections were held in support of the Spanish cause.

In July 1938, groups of refugee children arrived in South Wales. Mrs Rosa Steel worked in the Basque Children's Home in Swansea. Interviewed in 1985, she described how traumatised the children had been when they arrived. They were terrified of aeroplanes flying overhead and, as she describes, built shelters:

'Well, one day I was in one of the dormitories and I found that there were blankets missing... So, one of the little boys ... said "they're in the shelter". I said "shelter ... what shelter?" He said "this way, Mama Rosa", they used to call me Mama Rosa, of course, and he took me up to ... a little bit of wood, and there was a tunnel ... two tunnels, must've been about three yards apart, and well camouflaged with brushwood and shrubs. And he said to me "crawl under there Mama Rosa". So I crawled and it was like an entrance to an igloo you know... But it went down to about four or five feet down. And there they were, shelters! And they were there because they were terrified of sleeping in the homes because they said they were too exposed being in the house ... that they felt safer underground. So down I crawled and I explained to them "you're in a peaceful country now, there's no need for all these shelters'.

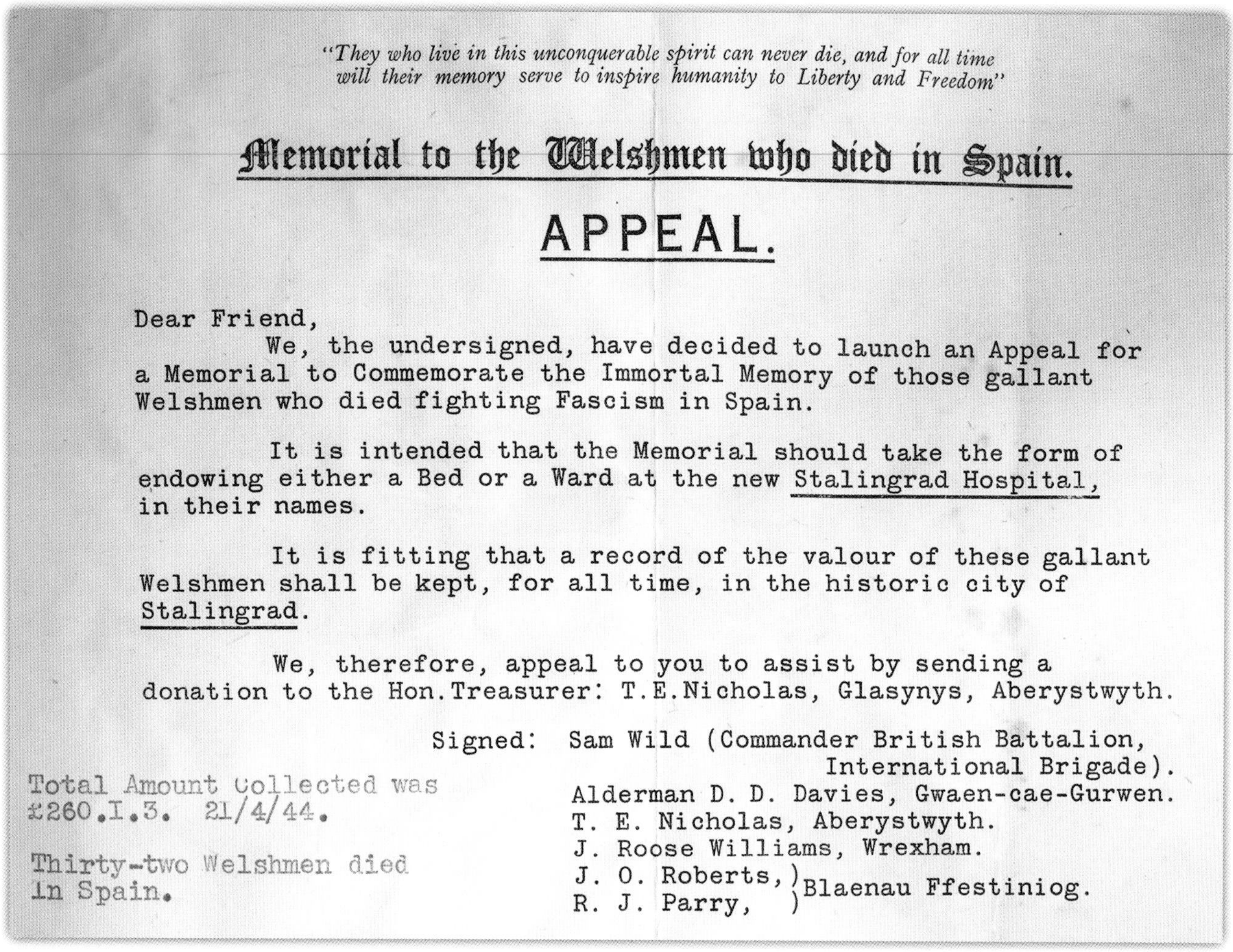

"They who live in this unconquerable spirit can never die, and for all time will their memory serve to inspire humanity to Liberty and Freedom"

Memorial to the Welshmen who died in Spain.

APPEAL.

Dear Friend,

We, the undersigned, have decided to launch an Appeal for a Memorial to Commemorate the Immortal Memory of those gallant Welshmen who died fighting Fascism in Spain.

It is intended that the Memorial should take the form of endowing either a Bed or a Ward at the new Stalingrad Hospital, in their names.

It is fitting that a record of the valour of these gallant Welshmen shall be kept, for all time, in the historic city of Stalingrad.

We, therefore, appeal to you to assist by sending a donation to the Hon. Treasurer: T.E.Nicholas, Glasynys, Aberystwyth.

Signed: Sam Wild (Commander British Battalion, International Brigade).
Alderman D. D. Davies, Gwaen-cae-Gurwen.
T. E. Nicholas, Aberystwyth.
J. Roose Williams, Wrexham.
J. O. Roberts,) Blaenau Ffestiniog.
R. J. Parry,)

Total Amount collected was £260.I.3. 21/4/44.

Thirty-two Welshmen died in Spain.

THE BOOK
OF THE
XV BRIGADE

RECORDS OF BRITISH, AMERICAN, CANADIAN, AND IRISH VOLUNTEERS IN THE XV INTERNATIONAL BRIGADE IN SPAIN
1936 - 1938

[handwritten inscription]

Published by the Commissariat of War, XV Brigade
MADRID, 1938

Above: This annotated letter of appeal for a memorial to the Welshmen who died in Spain in the new Stalingrad Hospital can be found inside T. E. Nicholas' copy of the book *Britons in Spain: the history of the British Batallion of the XVth International Brigade* by William Rust. It was published by Lawrence and Wishart in 1939.

Left: *The Book of the XV Brigade* was inscribed to T. E. Nicholas by Sam Wild, the Commander of the British Battalion of the International Brigade.

These books were donated to the South Wales Miners' Library by T. E. Nicholas' son, the historian, Islwyn Nicholas.

Next two pages: Spanish Civil War posters bequeathed to the South Wales Miners' Library by Tom Jones (Twm Sbaen).

los "patriotas" cien por cien entre gan España y sus fuentes de rique za al fascismo internacional

A LA GUERRA POR NUESTRA INDEPENDENCIA

JUNTA DELEGADA DE DEFENSA DE MADRID

DELEGACION DE PROPAGANDA Y PRENSA

QUE TU FAMILIA NO VIVA EL DRAMA DE LA GUERR

EVACUAR MADRID

ES AYUDAR A LA VICTORIA FINA

1940s: WORLD WAR AND THE DAWN OF A NEW ERA

The Second World War saw a dramatic increase in the demand for coal. During the War, the coal industry had been under Government control. The Labour Party won the General Election in 1945, and in 1946 introduced the Coal Nationalisation Act.

The new Risca Lodge banner proclaimed that the nationalisation of the coal industry on the 1st January 1947 was the 'Dawn of a New Era'.

The formation of the National Coal Board (NCB) did much to change the coal industry in South Wales for the better with improved health and safety and pit head baths.

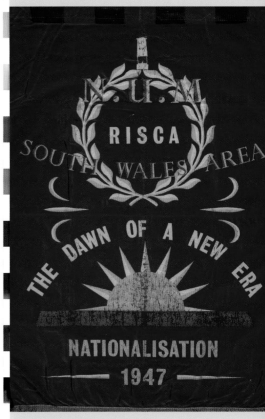

Risca Lodge had a banner made to mark nationalisation.

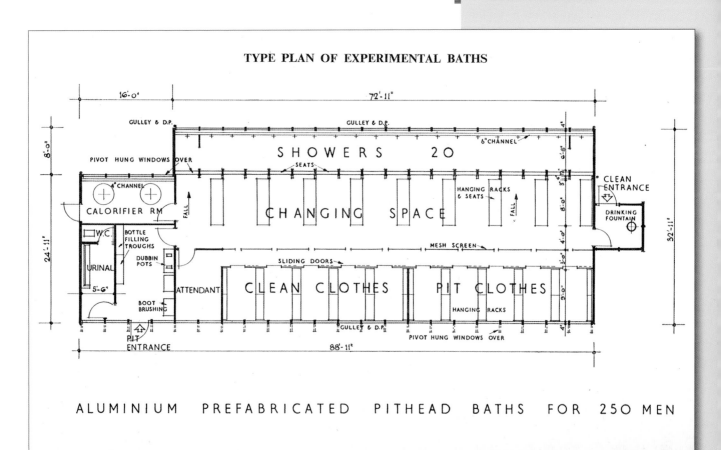

Extract from the Miners Welfare Fund Report from 1948 showing a plan of pithead baths big enough to accommodate 250 men. (Courtesy of the Coal Industries Social Welfare Organisation)

MINERS!

YOU HOLD THE KEY TO EUROPE

OPEN UP

VICTORY NEEDS COAL

Based on a design by IDRIS GRIFFITHS · NATIONAL COLLIERY · SOUTH WALES

The NCB and the National Union of Mineworkers (NUM), which had succeeded the Miners' Federation of Great Britain in 1945, worked together to improve safety in the industry. The system of wage payments also improved, with national wage agreements in 1956 and 1966.

Reg Fine of Maerdy, worked as a surfaceman at the time of nationalisation. In his opinion, nationalisation brought

> '...a better spirit you know. You know the men felt that at last they had got something that our fathers and we had fought for years and years to own our pits... I think we did feel better at that time. But of course mind you at that time the pressure was on the mines too. There was a big demand for coal, the pressure was on you see and the mines had been left in a terrible condition with the coal owners you see, terrible conditions. The machinery was outdated, old fashioned machinery and whatever machines they had was worn out and they never replaced them, and they were practically starting from scratch when the NCB took over you know'.

The South Wales Area of the NUM also developed its role within the mining communities. Two important initiatives were the creation of the Miners' Eisteddfod in 1948 and the Miners' Gala in 1954.

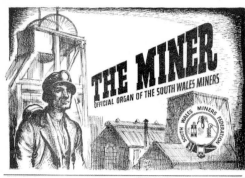

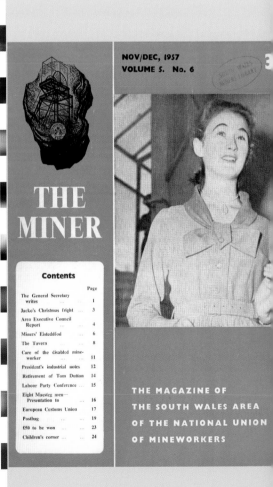

Top, Right: *The Miner*, published by the South Wales Miners' Federation, devoted its August 1946 issue to the work of the Talygarn Miners' Rehabilitation Centre. Opened in 1923, it became part of the Miners' Welfare Commission in 1943 and then part of the National Health Service in 1951.
(Courtesy of the National Union of Mineworkers, South Wales Area)

Bottom Right: The South Wales Area of the National Union of Mineworkers published *The Miner* in a magazine format between 1953 and in 1965.
(Courtesy of the National Union of Mineworkers, South Wales Area)

Opposite Page: One of the posters dating from World War II held in the South Wales Miners' Library.

Dai Francis, who was a member of the South Wales Area Executive Council in the 1940s described how,

'...Dai Dan Evans and one or two others went up to Durham and ... they came back and they thought, well we couldn't organise anything on the scale of the Miners' Gala in Durham because that was a hundred years old anyway. But perhaps we could organise a cultural event such as the Miners' Eisteddfod. Now that's how the Miners' Eisteddfod came into being. It was established to fill in that kind of cultural gap that was in the lives of the mining community as a result of the last war'.

The first Miners' Eisteddfod was held in the Grand Pavilion, Porthcawl in 1948 and sought to stimulate a range of cultural activities.

Those who attended the tenth Miners' Eisteddfod on 5 October 1957 at the Grand Pavilion, heard Paul Robeson sing to them live via a transatlantic telephone link from a secret recording studio in New York. Paul Robeson's passport had been withdrawn by the US Government in July 1950. As one of the prominent campaigners for the return of his passport, the South Wales Area NUM Executive Council had extended an invitation to Paul Robeson to attend their Eisteddfod every year since 1953.

Will Paynter told Paul Robeson, 'We look forward to the day when we shall shake your hand and hear you sing with all of us in these valleys of music and song'. Robeson responded with 'Thank you for those kind words. My warmest greetings to the people of my beloved Wales and a special hello to the miners of South Wales at your great festival. It is a privilege to be participating in this historic festival. All the best to you as we strive for a world where we can live abundant and dignified lives'.

Despite the Executive Council's initial reservations about the feasibility of establishing a Miners' Gala, the success of a demonstration in Cardiff in 1953 against section sixty-two of the Employment Act, saw the introduction of the annual Miners' Gala on 19 June 1954.

The NUM sold copies of the Transatlantic Exchange recording. (Courtesy of the National Union of Mineworkers, South Wales Area and Susan Robeson)

Opposite page: The first programme for the Gala Day, held in June 1954 .

(And following page: The programme for the South Wales Miners' Eisteddfod, held at the Grand Pavilion, Porthcawl on 5 October 1957.)

WELSH MINERS' FIRST ANNUAL GALA DAY

SOPHIA GARDENS CARDIFF
SATURDAY 19TH JUNE 1954

Miners on the march, October, 1953

Speakers today will be

THE RT. HON. ANEURIN BEVAN
P.C., M.P. (M.P. for Ebbw Vale)

Mr. A. L. HORNER,
General Secretary, N.U.M.

Chairman :   **Mr. W. PAYNTER, President,**
South Wales Area, N.U.M.

Programme 6d.

Proceeds in aid of Mineworkers' Benevolent Fund.

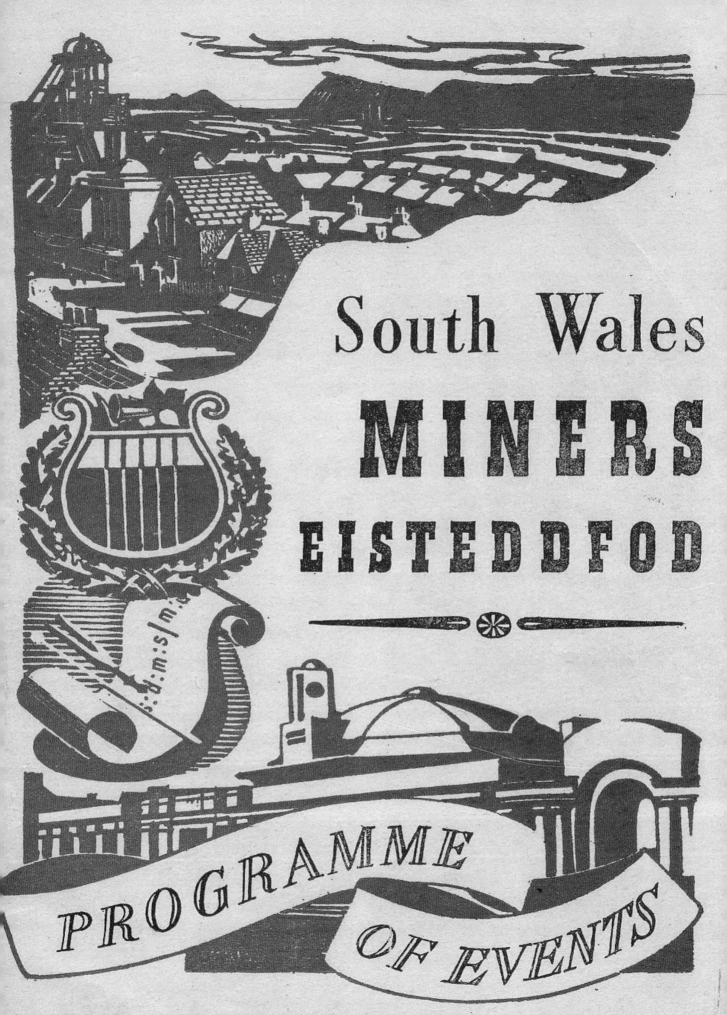

South Wales

MINERS

EISTEDDFOD

PROGRAMME

OF EVENTS

PRICE SIXPENCE.

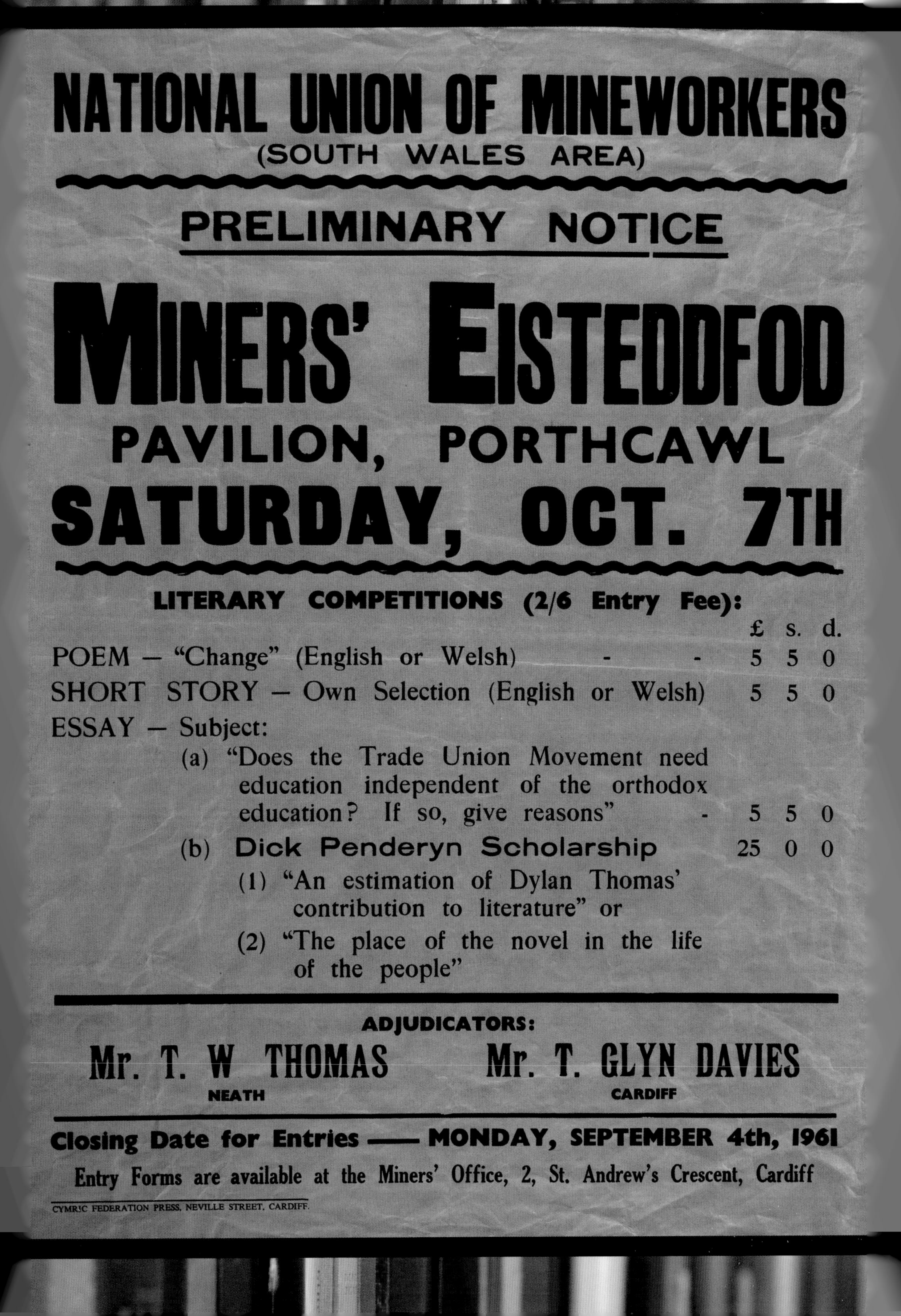

NATIONAL UNION OF MINEWORKERS
(SOUTH WALES AREA)

PRELIMINARY NOTICE

MINERS' EISTEDDFOD
PAVILION, PORTHCAWL
SATURDAY, OCT. 7TH

LITERARY COMPETITIONS (2/6 Entry Fee):

	£	s.	d.
POEM — "Change" (English or Welsh)	5	5	0
SHORT STORY — Own Selection (English or Welsh)	5	5	0
ESSAY — Subject:			
(a) "Does the Trade Union Movement need education independent of the orthodox education? If so, give reasons"	5	5	0
(b) Dick Penderyn Scholarship	25	0	0
(1) "An estimation of Dylan Thomas' contribution to literature" or			
(2) "The place of the novel in the life of the people"			

ADJUDICATORS:

Mr. T. W THOMAS
NEATH

Mr. T. GLYN DAVIES
CARDIFF

Closing Date for Entries —— MONDAY, SEPTEMBER 4th, 1961

Entry Forms are available at the Miners' Office, 2, St. Andrew's Crescent, Cardiff

CYMRIC FEDERATION PRESS, NEVILLE STREET, CARDIFF.

London March of South Wales miners in January 1959 led by Dai Dan Evans, whose interviews, books and pamphlets are housed in the South Wales Miners' Library; Jack Jones, who served in the International Brigades; and Garfield Rogers, who deposited the Cambrian NUM Lodge banner at the Library. (Courtesy of *The Times*)

Previous Page: A poster advertising the Miners' Eisteddfod in the Pavilion, Porthcawl in 1961. (Courtesy of the National Union of Mineworkers, South Wales Area)

THE 1960S: A DARK DECADE

The 1960s was a dark and disgraceful decade, deeply scarred by the terrible disasters of Aberfan, Six Bells, Cambrian and Tower collieries, as well as mass pit closures across the South Wales valleys, including Duffryn Rhondda in the Afan Valley in November 1966, recalled below by the poet Bryn Griffiths.

The colliery has closed this day,
bringing to a bleak end the long years
in the lamp-starred darkness,
and the miners now wander blindly
into another darkness of despair.

(There is no other work or future here.)

They will stand at street corners again,
telling of old friends and the dead days
forever gone into buried memory,
and they will know, forty years later,
a new depression, born of progress,
settling to slag the mind's
worn landscape with familiar despair.
But still they will sing,
the flashing wit melting into one
with the sudden shafts of autumn sunlight,
knowing of the close comradeship
which has always been theirs.

from 'The Death of Duffryn Rhondda'.
Taken from *Scars*, Dent, 1969.

THE MINER

MAGAZINE OF THE SOUTH WALES AREA NATIONAL UNION OF MINEWORKERS

2 ST. ANDREW'S CRESCENT, CARDIFF   Telephone 28776.   **SEPT/OCT 1960**

The General Secretary writes:

AGAIN BELLS TOLLED FOR THE SIX BELLS COLLIERY . . .
. . . for the real price of coal

Photograph by courtesy of "Coal" magazine

ON a beautiful summer's day, death struck silently, but relentlessly, in the bowels of the earth at this colliery and claimed 45 of our members as victims in this terrible disaster.

The mothers, daughters, sweethearts and relatives of the entombed men gathered around the pit top, along with thousands of others, seeking the latest news of their loved ones.

Rescue teams worked unstintingly and courageously in relays, advancing ahead of the working party. Their reports were eagerly awaited by H.M. Inspectorate, Union representatives and the Coal Board staff. One stood in amazement and wonderment at the cool manner in which these brave men reported on their findings, as they took to this work in a matter-of-fact manner which reflected great self possession and control. There was no room for panic in this situation.

Information was telephoned from the seat of the operations below ground to the colliery office, and directions were given for the next step to be taken in dealing with the situation. The well co-ordinated work resembled that of a crisis war operation. No man stinted but gave of his time, knowledge and courage in his endeavour to rescue the men.

1

Six Bells Colliery Disaster

Shortly after 10.45am on Tuesday 28 June 1960, the hooter sounded at Six Bells Colliery, Abertillery. An explosion had occurred underground in an area where forty-eight men were at work. The rescue teams rushed to the site, but, despite their best efforts, only three of the men survived. The resulting Inspector of Mines inquiry concluded that the probable cause of the explosion was firedamp ignited by a spark from a stone striking a metal canopy.

The loss of forty-five lives signified this tragedy as one of the worst post-war colliery disasters in the UK.

In his tribute (opposite), Dai Dan Evans wrote of all the messages of sympathy which poured in from around the world. Interviewed in November 1973, Mr O. Edwards, a union official from Markham spoke about his involvement in the aftermath of the disaster. He said,

> '...Six Bells, that was the greatest tragedy, the one which I can never forget however long I live ... although ... I did get a certain pleasure that I was able to assist people who had to go through this. I negotiated with the Coal Board for damages. I helped them get everything through the County Courts. I did everything I could for them. I arranged with the Ministry that they should have advances and all that... I found that [the authorities] from top to bottom were wonderful ... anything they could do they would, and I will be quite honest, I never saw a discordant note all the way'.

Dai Dan Evans, the General Secretary of the South Wales Area NUM wrote a tribute to the miners that were killed in the September–October 1960 edition of *The Miner*. (Courtesy of NUM South Wales Area)

Aberfan Disaster

On the morning of Friday 21 October 1966, a waste tip slid down the mountainside in Aberfan, near Merthyr Tydfil. The slide destroyed several houses in its path and engulfed Pantglas Junior School. 144 people died in the Aberfan disaster: 116 of them were school children. About half of the children at Pantglas Junior School, and five of their teachers, were killed.

On the twentieth anniversary of the disaster, a radio documentary *Aberfan: An Unknown Spring* was broadcast. A copy of the broadcast and the interviews conducted with people affected, including teachers and parents of victims, was given to the South Wales Miners' Library.

Amongst the material held in the South Wales Miners' Library about the Aberfan Disaster is a collection of interviews recorded for the BBC radio documentary *Aberfan: An Unknown Spring*, broadcast on the twentieth anniversary of the disaster in 1986. Included is a recording of the *Aberfan Thank You Show*, which was a performance made by the surviving children.

The Library has a large collection of newspaper cuttings dating from the 1920s to the 1990s. It includes cuttings about the 1966 disaster and its aftermath from the national daily newspapers.

1970S: 'TWO SWEET VICTORIES'

On 9 January 1972, 280,000 members of the National Union of Mineworkers (NUM) went on strike: the first national miners' struggle since 1926. In Wales, all the pits came to a standstill. The dispute was over pay. The miners were one of the lowest paid of all the skilled workers in the country, so at the NUM Conference in 1971, it was agreed to ask the National Coal Board for a pay rise. The Government refused to meet their demands. A month into the strike, a state of emergency was declared and a three day working week was introduced in an effort to save electricity.

The strike lasted for seven weeks, with the miners returning to work as one of the highest wage earners, and knowing that the general public realised how important coal was to the country's economy.

One of the striking miners, Dane Hartwell, interviewed in 1982, acknowledged the support of the public and other unions during the strike:

> '..[we] had a terrific amount of public support in 1972 because the wages were depressed... It was a very justifiable strike. I think the public were aware of it, and the support came from other trade unions too... The miners' victory of '72, of course, was a victory for the trade union movement in general; for the workers in Great Britain then, and for the trade union movement in general – just showing what can be done'.

14

National Union of Mineworkers
(SOUTH WALES AREA)

MINUTES of Special Area Conference, held at The Casino, Porthcawl, on Friday, 7th January, 1972.

PRESENT.

Mr. Glyn Williams, President.
Mr. Emlyn Williams, Vice-President.
Mr. D. Francis, General Secretary.
Mr. Ben Morris, Chief Administrative Officer.
Executive Council Members, Miners' Agents and delegates from each lodge in the South Wales Coalfield.
Mr. Glyn Williams presided.

Agenda :

Wage Negotiations.

The President welcomed delegates to this important Conference and reviewed the background to the present dispute and also briefly the position as he reported it at the last Area Annual Conference.

He stated that the most recent developments were that a meeting had been held between the National Officials and the Board on Tuesday, 4th January. It was stressed that this meeting was not a negotiating meeting, but merely a meeting to find out if there was a basis or a formula that would avoid a National strike.

The full National Executive Committee met on Wednesday, 5th January, and after some discussion they agreed to meet representatives of the Coal Board, who attended for the meeting at the N.U.M. Offices, London.

The Board had stated that they had again addressed themselves to this question, and the maximum they could offer was £2 a week increase "across the Board," for all Daywage workmen and £1.90 for N.P.L.A. Third Structure men and others. They stated also that they were prepared to give an additional week's holiday. This week's holiday not to be taken on a collective basis, but taken on the same basis as now applied to individual rest days. Three could be taken before November, 1972, and the further two probably around the Christmas period.

Minutes of the NUM South Wales Area Special Area Conference 7 January 1972, held to discuss the current situation regarding wage negotiations with the National Coal Board.

A march through Cardiff during the 1974 strike. (Courtesy of Hywel Francis)

Despite the victory, two years later, the miners found themselves again in dispute with the Government over pay, and the miners voted to go out on strike on 9 February 1974. Once again, a state of emergency and a three day working week were declared.

The Prime Minister, Edward Heath, called a General Election for 28 February, in the belief that the electorate would support the Government, but the Conservative Party was defeated.

As Alec Jones, MP for Rhondda from 1967 to 1983 commented,

'...and when Heath went to the country

I don't think he went to the country out of the kindness of his heart, what he went to the country on at that time was because he thought he was going to win, that he could beat the miners, come back with a larger majority and carry on for a long period of time. But it just didn't happen of course. But I think it didn't happen because he didn't realise the amount of feeling which there was throughout the country, basically in favour of the miners'.

Within weeks, the new Labour Government had reached a deal with the miners and the strike ended.

Opposite: Poster produced by the NUM during the 1972 strike.
(Courtesy of the National Union of Mineworkers, South Wales Area)

Neil Kinnock, the MP for Bedwellty during the strikes, referred to them in 1980 as 'two sweet victories'. However, he reflected on the fact that,

> '...in the course of those strikes people went through an enormous political experience. There were fellows reading five and six newspapers a day sitting with ten or twelve other blokes .... and they went through terrific experiences, some of that's rubbed off and some have retained that political commitment, but it died away quickly, immediately after the strikes. It was never capitalised on by the Labour Party or by any other party, certainly not by the NUM and that's a great shame. I think we will pay a big price for that. [However] ... these two stark events for a new generation of miners did encourage the development of a new younger leadership, there's no question about that...'

In an effort to encourage this development of new leaders, in 1975, the first trade union Day Release course was held at the South Wales Miners' Library in cooperation with Swansea University's Extra-Mural Department, the NUM and the TUC.

'A Strike-breaker is a traitor'

Blacklegs in the Garw Valley of South Wales in 1929.

Jack London's definition of a Scab.

'After God had finished the rattlesnake, the toad and vampire, He had some awful substance left with which he made a scab.

'A scab is a two-legged animal with a cork-screw soul, a water-logged brain, a combination backbone of jelly and glue. Where others have a heart, he carries a tumour of rotten principles.

'When a scab comes down the street, men turn their backs, the angels weep in heaven, and the Devil shuts the gates of Hell to keep him out.

'No man has a right to scab so long as there is a pool of water to drown his carcass in, or a rope long enough to hang his body with. Judas Iscariot was a gentleman compared with a scab, for after betraying his Master he had character enough to hang himself. A scab has not.

'Esau sold his birthright for a mess of pottage. Judas Iscariot sold his Saviour for 30 pieces of silver. Benedict Arnold sold his country for the promise of a commission in the British Army. The modern strike-breaker sells his birthright, his country, his wife, his children and his fellow-men for an unfilled promise from his employer.

'Esau was a traitor to himself; Judas Iscariot was a traitor to his God; Benedict Arnold was a traitor to his country. A STRIKE-BREAKER IS A TRAITOR to his God, his country, his wife, his family and his class. A REAL MAN NEVER BECOMES A STRIKE-BREAKER . . . .'

Leaflet produced by the NUM South Wales Area during the early part of the 1984–5 strike.

1980s and 1990s: 'The NUM fights for Wales'

Even in the difficult decade of decline in the 1980s, the South Wales Miners' Library continued to be that 'citadel' as Will Paynter called it in 1983: a citadel of learning, resistance, retrieval and reflection. The Rhondda writer Gwyn Thomas, who had been a sterling supporter of the Library and its educational work, had died in 1981, and his widow Lyn, decided to donate his collection of books, notebooks and posters to the Library.

Posters advertising Gwyn Thomas plays.

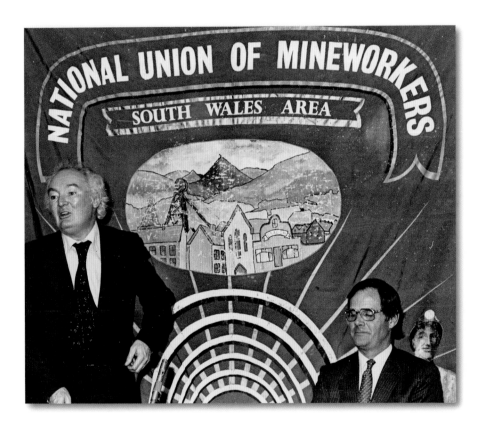

The poet and film-maker John Ormond (above left) speaking at the tenth anniversary of the South Wales Miners' Library on the occasion of the presentation of the Gwyn Thomas Library. On the right is the Principal of the University, Professor Brian Clarkson. (Courtesy of the South Wales Coalfield Collection, Swansea University)

In 1983, Friends of the Library presented a painting by Valerie Ganz of Brynlliw Colliery to mark the Library's tenth anniversary.

The writer Alun Richards, teaching in the Bargoed Room at of the South Wales Miners' Library. In the background is the portrait of William Abraham (Mabon) MP of Rhondda (1885–95) and first president of the South Wales Miners' Federation (1898–1912). The portrait was bequeathed to the South Wales Miners' Library by the NUM South Wales Area. (Courtesy of Hywel Francis)

The Valleys' Star was sometimes produced during the 1984–5 strike in the South Wales Miners' Library by Tim Exton.

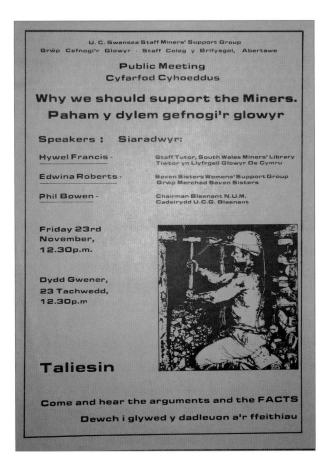

By 1984, the coal industry was in crisis. There were only twenty-eight collieries left in South Wales. On 6 March 1984, the NCB put forward proposals to eliminate twenty thousand British mining jobs and a further twenty thousand jobs in related industries and services. Cortonwood Colliery in South Yorkshire was the first to be closed. The effect of these plans in South Wales meant that over half of the male population in mining communities would be out of work with little prospect of alternative work in their locality.

A member of the Cwm Llantwit Women's Support Group said:

> 'There would be seven people working on our street if the Cwm shut tomorrow – out of a street of fifty-two.'

On 12 March, 1984, the NUM called a national strike against the pit closures.

The year long strike was one of the most bitter and hard fought industrial disputes Britain has ever seen, involving the government, the police, the press and the NUM. Mining communities faced hardship as they struggled to save their jobs and their communities. NUM funds were confiscated and police intervened to allow strike breakers to go to work.

Author Menna Gallie speaking at the Women's Day School at Onllwyn Miners' Welfare Hall on 25 May 1985. It was organised by the Neath, Dulais and Swansea Valley Miners' Support Group. A recording of the event is held in the South Wales Miners' Library. (Courtesy of Hywel Francis)

In October 2013, the Manic Street Preachers used footage of the Neath, Dulais and Swansea Valley Miners' Support Group held at the South Wales Miners' Library in the video for their single 'Anthem for a Lost Cause'.

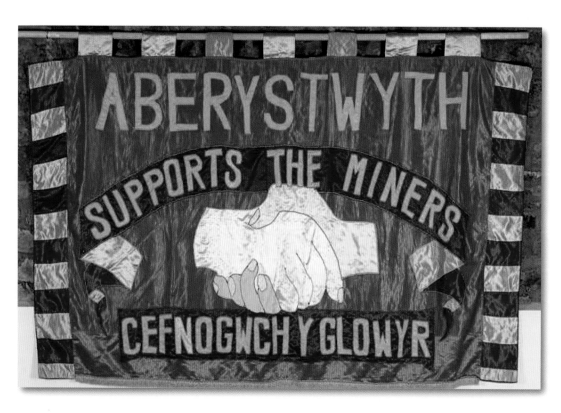

Left: Banner maker Thalia Campbell deposited the Aberystwyth Supports the Miners banner at the South Wales Miners' Library in 2005. (Courtesy of Siân Williams)

Poster advertising a concert in London to raise funds for the striking miners in South Wales.

There was much support for the striking miners in South Wales. The miners' wives played a crucial role. In many communities, the women formed Women's Support Groups, through which they organised food parcels, soup kitchens and organised Christmas appeals for the children. They joined the picket lines alongside the men, addressed rallies and proudly marched behind their banners bearing slogans such as 'Women Against Pit Closures'.

One activist recalled,

'In a little community like this (Maerdy), if you've got someone living next door, if it's an old age pensioner or someone in work, and you've got a family, they won't watch you starve. But we agreed in the committee that if anyone had nothing in the house that they can just come along and ask for more food'.

Support for the striking miners also came from other parts of the country. Elvis Costello, Billy Bragg and the Flying Pickets showed their support by appearing in fundraising concerts, such as the one in London in 1985.

The Wales Congress in Support of Mining Communities was set up during the strike as an initiative of the South Wales Area NUM in order to coordinate solidarity across and beyond Wales. At the end of the strike, the Congress produced an exhibition to portray some of the struggles the Welsh miners had faced.

The exhibition was unveiled at the National Eisteddfod in Rhyl in 1985 and then toured throughout Wales before becoming part of the South Wales Miners' Library's collection.

After the strike ended, it became clear that the original closure programme would become more extensive, with fifty collieries to close along with fifty thousand jobs.

In South Wales, the mass closures of collieries meant that by 1991, mining employment had been virtually wiped out.

On 19 April 1994, Tower Colliery, the last deep mine in South Wales closed. However, believing the mine to be profitable, the miners, led by Tyrone O'Sullivan, bought the pit. It was kept in production until, finally exhausted, it closed in 2008.

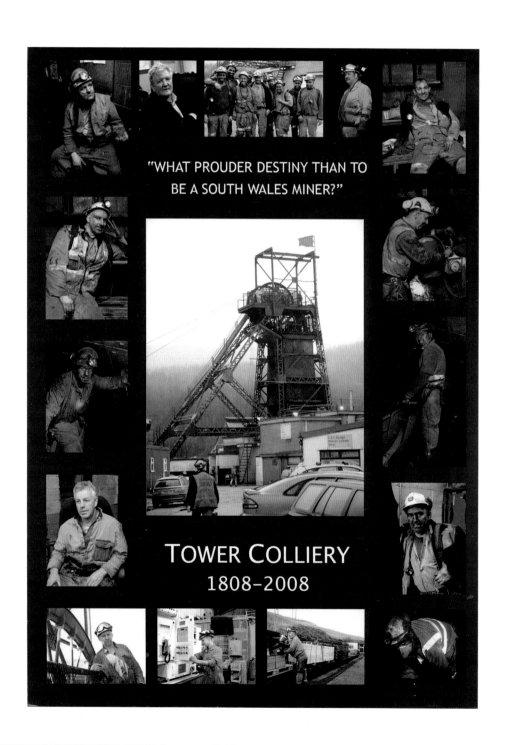

"WHAT PROUDER DESTINY THAN TO BE A SOUTH WALES MINER?"

TOWER COLLIERY
1808–2008

Leaflet produced by Tower Colliery just before it closed in 2008. (Courtesy of Tower Colliery)

In 1990, Elaine Morgan, the Welsh television dramatist and author presented copies of the video tapes of her plays to the Library as part of a scheme organised by Alun Richards to gather materials relating to Welsh writers with connections to the valleys and the South Wales Miners' Library.

Four years later, Elaine Morgan became an Honorary Fellow of Swansea University. During the ceremony, Hywel Francis referred to her long association with the Department of Adult Continuing Education as a lecturer on their Film and Drama courses.

With her husband Morien Morgan, a former International Brigader, Elaine was an enthusatic supporter of the memorial to the Welshmen killed during the Spanish Civil War at the South Wales Miners' Library. An oral history interview with Morien Morgan is held in the Library.

Elaine Morgan was awarded an Honorary Fellowship of Swansea University on 11 July 1994. She is pictured after the ceremony with (L–R) Hywel Francis, Professor Brian Clarkson (Principal), and Lord James Callaghan (Chancellor of the University). (Courtesy of Swansea University)

One of the banners used in the Yes campaign autographed by the leader in Scotland, the late Donald Dewar, and in Wales, Ron Davies. The banners were deposited at the South Wales Miners' Library as an acknowledgment of the pivotal role played by the NUM and by mining communities in the campaigns of 1979 and 1997. (Courtesy of Steve Howell)

YES FOR WALES

On 1 March 1979, the Labour Government held a referendum to determine whether a Welsh Assembly should be established, as proposed by the Kilbrandon Report. The proposals were defeated. During the following eighteen years when the Conservative Party were in Government, the arguments for devolution did not disappear. Following the Labour Party's victory at the General Election on 1 May 1997, a white paper was published 'A Voice for Wales', which outlined the new proposals for devolution.

After a hard fought campaign by both the 'Yes for Wales' and the 'No Campaign' supporters, the referendum on the 18 September 1997 saw 50.3% vote to support devolution.

The first Assembly elections were held on 6 May 1999 and on 26 May, the National Assembly for Wales opened in Cardiff.

As the twentieth century drew to a close, the South Wales Miners' Library looked to the new millennium with optimism. With only one deep mine left in South Wales, coalfield society had changed dramatically. However, the emerging new technologies of the last decade offered us new opportunities and challenges.

Enriching Lives

George Brinley Evans

'A big part of my Life'

Courtesy of Steve Williams

The first time I went to the South Wales Miners' Library in Maes-yr-Haf in Sketty, I was in the company of my friends Doug Millar, Jeff Camnant and Les Jones from the Dulais Valley.

We had arranged the visit especially to see the memorial to the men from South Wales, who had lost their lives fighting with the International Brigades against Franco.

Three names stood out for me. Frank Zamora; his brother had worked as a collier boy with my father. Victoriano Esteban because I had worked with a Mr Esteban in the Rhas Drift, who I think was Victoriano's grandfather, he was old and as tough as old boots, and Harold James Strangward. I knew his brother George.

By now I was no longer a miner, having lost an eye in an accident on Will Fry's heading in the Cornish Drift Onllwyn No. 3, but was still a member of the NUM, and was pleased and proud that the union I belonged to had publicly honoured the courage of these brave young men who had made the ultimate sacrifice in the defence of Europe's freedom.

It did not occur to me then that the South Wales Miners' Library was going to play a very important part in my life over the next forty years.

While convalescing and moaning about the programmes on television, my wife, Peg told me, 'You're spoiling it for everyone. Shut up, and if you think you can write something better, do it!' I did, in long hand. Peg bought a typewriter and as I could not type Peg got Carol, who was courting John the Bake House, to type it, and without telling me, sent it off to the BBC.

Weeks later Peg handed me a letter. It was from Harry Green, one of the BBC's leading scriptwriters, originally from Neath, inviting me to the Television Centre in London on 9 March 1962, my son Owen's birthday. Everything was frozen solid.

I still had not been fitted with an artificial eye because of a persistent infection in my eye socket. 'You'd better let the doctor know' said Peg.

I walked up to see Doctor Thomas. He and Mrs Thomas were delighted. 'Is George well enough to go to London, Dafydd? I'll telephone Donald Alexander. He'll keep an eye on George'. Donald Alexander was a documentary filmmaker and had been at university with the doctor.

I had written a script for television, *The Fourth Device*, a drama taking place in the darkness of a coalmine, but television was still in black and white. 'I asked you to London, George, because of all the scripts I've received this is one of the best written. Take it home and put it between two cardboard covers', said Harry Green over a cup of tea.

Eventually with the help of George Ewart Evans, my story 'Boys of Gold' was published in the *Anglo Welsh Review* in 1978. I was working for Bewley & John, then on to Roadville, then to Gemark and finally to Wimpy Mining and retirement; there had been no time for writing. I was now on my own as Peg had died. Doug Miller turned up saying, 'George, this new place they've opened, the DOVE, there's a top tutor there, Alun Richards. You can't stay here on your own!' I took Doug's advice and met Alun Richards for the first time. I had read his book, *The Former Miss Merthyr Tydfil*. Each week Alun gave us a short story to read by a famous author from the well stocked shelves of the South Wales' Miners Library, now with a branch at the DOVE, Banwen. 'George, you didn't tell me you'd been published!' He gave the class 'Boys of Gold' and thankfully they liked it. 'George, send something to Short Story Wales to that *Cambrensis* editor chap called Arthur Smith.' I did and 'The Man Who Stayed a Miner' was published in March 1996.

Arthur Smith was fascinated with the DOVE and asked for an article on it. I persuaded Mandy Orford who worked in the Banwen branch of the South Wales Miners' Library to write it. Arthur was delighted with her work and telephoned me to ask for a photograph of Mandy to go with the article.

Arthur wrote and asked me to contribute to an anthology that he and Parthian were bringing out titled, *Mama's Baby (Papa's Maybe)*. I did. Then Parthian asked me to write seven short stories. I did. It was titled *Boys of Gold* and then I wrote *Where The Flying Fishes Play*.

The art historian Barry Plummer sent me a letter and a photograph of Evan Walters' portrait of a Welsh miner asking me would I write about it. I told Mandy Orford at the South Wales Miners' Library and the following week I had the information and was able to write the article, which was published in Barry Plummer's *Moments of Vision*.

On my 86th birthday in November 2012, I was invited to the South Wales Miners' Library in Hendrefoelan to unveil the two paintings I had given them as a very small thank you for the tremendous help given to me by the staff of the South Wales Miners' Library. The paintings were 'The Death of Silver', that gained a place at the twelfth International Art Exhibition at Warwick Square in London 1967, and 'Cogging in the Four Feet', which was used as the cover of *Boys of Gold*. Parthian gave the South Wales Miners' Library a complete set of its Library of Wales series.

Tyrone O'Sullivan

'Influencing Working People in Wales and the World'

Courtesy of Swansea University

I will always remember the role played and importance of education in the National Union of Mineworkers (NUM), and the major role taken up by and through the South Wales Miners' Library in Swansea.

My first introduction was a full week day release course at the Library in 1975. The agenda was how to write, how to move, and how to support resolutions at Conferences. British Coal paid our wages for the week (if only they had realised it was a hotbed of politics and socialism!). On that first course with me was Des Dutfield, Terry Thomas, Arfon Evans, and Terry Davies. Of the twenty odd attending that first week, ninety percent of us went on to hold major posts in the National Union of Mineworkers (South Wales Area) and national positions playing leading roles in major strikes of the future, but also making major decisions and moving important Resolutions at Labour Party Conferences and TUC Conferences .

Yes, the South Wales Miners' Library through its education courses that continued years after we attended that first course influenced and benefitted working people not only in Wales, but the UK and the world.

RICHARD GREATREX

'THE SOUL OF THE SOUTH WALES MINERS' LIBRARY'

Courtesy of Richard Greatrex

It's 1974, January if I remember correctly. We're heading to Swansea. I have never experienced a miners' strike and John Gaventa hardly knows where South Wales is. Specifically we are heading to Maes-yr-Haf, a glorious, miniature Palladian building. It is imposing, should we step in? It holds, we are told, photos, banners, posters, oral history tapes and many books rescued from Miners' Institute Libraries.

But, for the moment, that's not what we have travelled from Oxford for. We want to know where to go, we want directions.

Inside we meet Hywel Francis, wise beyond his twenty-eight years and Dai Smith, pugnacious as ever at twenty-nine. There must have been others of course, but it is Hywel and Dai who I remember.

Well it wasn't long before John and myself had been introduced to so many of those involved with the conflict. From Dai Francis, leader of the South Wales NUM to Phil Weeks, South Wales Director of the NCB and in between Chris Evans, the man of many stories, Terry Thomas, Tyrone O'Sullivan, Kim Howells and so many others.

Yes, of course, it wasn't the imposing edifice of the South Wales Miners' Library that we needed, it was its soul and that is what we found. Its soul was its inhabitants: from the people, of the people and most importantly, knowing the people.

You ask of course how could these people help us? Well, we have the video equipment, an impossibly heavy video recorder hanging off my shoulder and the camera that seems the opposite of ergonomic. We need to video miners. John has this crazy idea to swap information between South Wales and Appalachia. He talks about "cultural exchange" and thinks the idea will catch on!

Turns out John was right. We spent as much time as possible in South Wales during the sixteen weeks of the dispute. Our aim was to video anything connected to the strike: be it a demonstration, a meeting, a picket line, an interview or even the television news. We had no clear intention for the material except that it may turn out to be useful in some future exchange. We also had no particular framework, no theory, about what we should record except that we knew which side we were on.

We ended up with hours of video footage and with 'cultural exchange' beckoning us we headed to the USA, video tapes in hand. Sure enough miners, miners' families, educators and organisers in Tennessee, Kentucky and West Virginia seemed interested. We compiled the material in different ways for different groups. We had in mind the idea of promoting debate rather than giving a lecture. Again it seemed to work.

It wasn't long before this kind of exchange developed further. In 1976 Helen Lewis and I moved to Brynamman in the Amman Valley and with regular visits from John, we developed the Welsh Tapes, a portrait of the area, again with the idea of exchanging ideas, experiences, history and myths.

And so it goes, to this day, this exchange.

And within it still, the soul of the South Wales Miners' Library.

ALUN BURGE

'A LIFELONG RELATIONSHIP'

Alun Burge interviewing Elvet Evans in Cwmfelinfach
on 4 January 1978. (Courtesy of South Wales
Coalfield Collection, Swansea University)

I first started using the Miners' Library in 1977 when it was in Maes-yr-Haf and still do, two
buildings and nearly four decades later, in Hendrefoelan. It continues to be the epitome of what a
public facing service should be: a brilliant place to work with the most welcoming staff.

In those days I was a postgraduate student fumbling towards research on the Nine Mile Point
Colliery, where my grandfather had worked, and on its twin communities of Cwmfelinfach and
Ynysddu. I had been in correspondence with Hywel Francis while an undergraduate at Hull
University and it was his support and encouragement, as well as the presence of the Library,
which helped bring me to Swansea.

While the only published outcome of that early period was an article on 'scabbing', it started
me on a lifelong relationship with the materials held in the Library, which is still evolving. At
different times I have used the collection to write articles on the role of the voluntary sector
in South Wales between the wars, on various aspects of adult learning in the coalfield, a piece
on the unedifying response of the labour movement to the introduction of African labour
in the Great War, as well as the more obvious subject of the differing characteristics of pre-
nationalisation coal companies. For most of the last decade I have been working on the history
of the co-operative movement in South Wales. These topics hint at the breadth of subjects that
can be fruitfully researched using Miners' Library sources. Of late I have suggested to others how
they can use the collection to research the Appalachian coalfield, as well as disability in South
Wales. The publications and reports held in the Library make it, along with the National Library
in Aberystwyth, by far the best collection on the co-operative movement in Wales.

The nature of the sources available in print, such as minutes, pamphlets and oral testimony,
is many and varied. However, the richness of the collection also lies in the way that it can

be used to change interpretations over time. Sometimes the sources which are not in the collection say as much as those that are. The collections policy of the 1970s would be (and is) quite different now. Equally my pre-1985 focus on strikes and riots instead of, say, sport, the co-operative society or St John's Ambulance, say as much about my context and me as they do about the topic. Questions about gender balance were not yet being posed (though I am pleased that more by luck than judgement my longest interview, with Mrs Elizabeth Roberts, of Cwmfelinfach, did include gender relationships and the decline of the Welsh language).

It is not possible to write this piece without referring to Llafur, which in the 1970s and early 1980s was a remarkable social force. Hywel Francis engagingly referred to Llafur as the political wing of the Miners' Library, which points to the umbilical relationship that existed between the two. As one Llafur committee member said, we thought we could change the world through a history society. It would be interesting to read the Special Branch files that might have been kept on us. I would hate to think they were too thin. Hopefully the Miners' Library, which was in effect Llafur's HQ, earned itself an honourable mention too.

Colin Trotman (front row, fourth from left) as a tutor on the NUM class in 1988. Also in the picture is Billy Pye (front row, third from left), then a miner St John's Colliery, Maesteg, and now the celebrated swimming Paralympic coach of gold winning medallist Ellie Symmonds.

COLIN TROTMAN

'A UNIQUE RESOURCE'

Colin Trotman (back row, centre) as an NUM student at the South Wales Miners' Library in 1980.

The Miners' Institute Libraries and subsequently the South Wales Miners' Library, which was established in October 1973 to coincide with the seventy-fifth anniversary of the founding of the South Wales Miners' Federation, have played a significant part in my personal development.

Born into a coalminer's family in Ammanford, in the heart of the anthracite belt, I was the son of the son of the son of a coalminer's son who eventually became a coalminer himself albeit a coalface electrician. I can only recall one male member of my extended family, on both my mother and father's side, who was not a coalminer. The town of Ammanford, like coal mining towns across the South Wales Coalfield, had its Miners' Institute. My earliest contact with the Institute was as the youngest member of a family group of cousins, older than I, who discovered that the Miners' Institute contained two full size snooker tables. We were desperate to use them and we often sneaked in but equally so we were caught by the doorman. He invariably refused us entry to the snooker facility but always, without fail, encouraged us to use the reading room and library. I can only honestly claim to have gone into the reading room. Little was I to know the Miners' Institute Libraries would loom large in my later life history.

At fifteen years of age I ditched my family's hopes and aspirations for me by 'quitting' Grammar School and taking up an electrical apprenticeship with the then National Coal Board. For the next fourteen years I plied my trade in Cwmgwili Colliery and for a shorter period at the New Betws Mine. During my time at Cwmgwili I was elected as Craftsman's Representative on the National Union of Mineworkers' South Wales Area (NUM) Lodge Committee and subsequently, attended the union's day release programme organised by the Extra Mural Department at Swansea University. As a result, I was exposed to not only the collection of institute libraries at Maes-yr-Haf and later at Hendrefoelan but also to a wealth of literature and political personalities. Bert Coombes *These Poor Hands*, Orwell's

Road to Wigan Pier, Raymond Williams, Gwyn Thomas, Karl Marx and R. H. Tawney amongst the better known authors and volume after volume from the Left Book Club in their red and sometimes orange garb. I have fond memories of my days on the NUM South Wales Area day release programme. Two of our tutors were ex-coalminers, another was the son of a past General Secretary of the South Wales Miners, another was later to become research officer for the South Wales NUM and both, much later, were to become Labour Members of Parliament for Pontypridd and Aberavon respectively.

That experience also provided me with an opportunity to meet and talk to some of the great political activists and Trades Union leaders. I well remember having lunch sitting opposite Dai Francis, General Secretary of the South Wales NUM. I was almost too nervous to eat but he put me at my ease. Through my time as a student on the NUM day release programme and during the time I was co-ordinating the day release programme, I was privileged to be able to listen to the likes of Jack Dunn (President Kent Coalfield), Mick MaGahey (Scottish Miners' Leader), John Monks (TUC), Emlyn Williams (President NUM South Wales Area), Jimmy Knapp (General Secretary of the National Union of Railwaymen) and many others.

Besides the direct impact the South Wales Miners' Library had upon me, I will never forget the sessions, as a part of that programme, whereby we were set free to research our own topics in the library at Swansea University. I well remember standing in the library, mouth almost agape, astounded by the number of books, the archives, the journals, so much written knowledge in one place. I knew there and then what I wanted to do next and that was to become an undergraduate. The intellectual unionism that was the collaboration between the Extra Mural Department at Swansea and the NUM South Wales Area gave me the opportunity to reassess and re-evaluate my educational needs. The rest, as my predecessor as head of the department, Professor Hywel Francis, might have said 'is history'. I entered Swansea as an undergraduate in 1981, graduated with a degree in Sociology in 1985, subsequently gained a PhD and in 1988 became a co-ordinating tutor for the very same day release programme of which I was myself a beneficiary.

Fifty years after I first stepped into the reading room in the Ammanford Miners' Institute I have a close working relationship with the South Wales Miners' Library. It was always a unique resource when it operated via the institutes, it became a unique collection and today remains unique. It figures significantly in my life history and forms a part of my heritage of which I am very proud. However, and perhaps more importantly, the South Wales Miners' Library lives and thrives. The community-based widening access work undertaken by my Department (of Adult Continuing Education) would not be possible without the resources, support and commitment of staff at the South Wales Miners' Library. The Miners' Library inspired a whole generation of young miners from 1974 to 1990. For some of us, it countered the educational alienation we suffered as a result of 'schooling' by reinvigorating in us a new thirst for learning, for knowledge.

CHRIS WILLIAMS

'MY FAVOURITE LIBRARY'

Courtesy of Chris Williams

I don't think there is any doubt that the South Wales Miners' Library is my favourite library in the world, its relevance, warmth and bustle just edging out the rarefied atmosphere and the scholarly glories of the Bodleian.

I started coming to work in the Miners' Library when I was a PhD student in the 1980s when it was located in Hendrefoelan House, run by the formidable Mrs Campbell. The sense of being 'in' history as well as studying history was very real, as one gazed up at the faded spines of Left Book Club editions or took dog-eared copies of socialist newspapers off the shelves. Studying the visitors' book was an education in itself, and one never knew who might stumble in (famous historian, television documentary maker, trade union leader). It was, and remains, the spiritual home of the world of Welsh labour history, where one can go hoping to get away from the normal pressures of the working week to pursue one's latest research project or enthusiasm. The delight of working in the modern library is not only the frequent supplies of instant coffee (occasionally supplemented by chocolates) or the opportunity to browse the bargain book trolley, but the fact that so much is there, in one relatively small building, and on open shelves too! In too many libraries and archives today there is no chance to browse, to stumble on the unanticipated but wonderful discovery, to speculate, as it were, intellectually, so the Miners' Library is a libertarian revelation. And the librarians are themselves walking card indexes, full of knowledge, memories, ideas and suggestions. Time spent in their company is never wasted. I have, for approaching thirty years, revelled in the fluid, fertile and above all friendly atmosphere of the South Wales Miners' Library, in its varying physical forms, and introduced cohort after cohort of undergraduate students to its treasures. It is one of Swansea University's USPs – unique selling points – and its value to the university, to scholarship and to South Wales more generally, should be proclaimed at every opportunity.

Mandy Orford

'The Miners' Library and Me'

I first heard of the South Wales Miners' Library whilst attending an IT course at the DOVE Workshop in Banwen in 1992. At that time I was employed at Tick Tock in Ystradgynlais, and I had no idea what the Miners' Library was all about. During my time at DOVE I had some guidance and completed the Adult Directions questionnaire: the results revealed that I would like to work in a library. The DOVE staff, Mair, Lesley and Julie were very encouraging, and arranged for me to volunteer at the library one day a week. I was then made aware of a part-time job vacancy at the Miners' Library and I was encouraged to apply. Siân Williams, the new Librarian at the Miners' Library, interviewed me and luckily she saw some potential and offered me the job. It was October 1995. Over the next ten years based in Hendrefoelan House, the Miners' Library went from strength to strength. We worked closely with the Department of Adult Continuing Education and developed many services to support their students on campus and out in the community. I worked at our branch library in Banwen, based in the DOVE Workshop, three days a week. I loved my job in both locations. At Banwen, I was responsible for the daily running of the library and I thrived on the challenge; I particularly enjoyed helping the students. At the Miners' Library I was able to be more involved with the South Wales Coalfield Collection and enquiries relating to mining history, and I began to realise the importance of the collection.

In 2006 the Miners' Library relocated to the Coach House on the Hendrefoelan Estate; this allowed the library to expand even further. We were able to open longer hours and regularly on weekends, we were able to have our collections more readily accessible and in one place and we finally had some teaching and IT rooms to offer classes. The library has embraced the technological revolution with many services becoming digital, online and downloadable, while still retaining our traditional lending. This has allowed the Miners' Library to provide an excellent service for all the staff, students and visitors we have.

The Miners' Library is a vibrant, friendly, relaxing and inspirational place to be. Many of our users have commented on the wonderful atmosphere, which is created by the building, the surroundings, the collections and the great staff. I am proud to be associated with the Miners' Library and it has given me more than just employment: it has opened my eyes to a whole culture and history I knew little about.

DENISE LEWIS

'A PEACEFUL HAVEN...'

Hywel Francis congratulating Denise Lewis
on her first-class honours degree in July
2012. (Courtesy of Mandy Orford)

I've lived in the Dulais Valley all my life. Whilst growing up it was a predominantly mining community. My father and three brothers all worked underground in the local colliery. I never felt that education was a priority; jobs were readily available and there seemed no reason to study.

University was never talked about within my circle of friends and when I left school I went to work in a local factory. Whilst working in the factory the employees were given the opportunity to take up free training, so I took a huge leap and enrolled on to a Pitman's word processing course at the DOVE Workshop in Banwen. School had never suited me, I always felt nervous and unsettled. However, DOVE was a non-threatening environment within which I thrived and it gave me the confidence and flexibility to continue doing various courses over a period of years.

I always felt unfulfilled educationally and therefore didn't have the confidence to apply for a job outside of the factory. After many years of part time study, in 1998 I applied for a part time degree, but my nervousness prevented me from attending the interview. In 2002, I was successful in obtaining an administrative assistant's job with Communities First (a Welsh Government anti-poverty initiative), which was based at DOVE. Two years later I gained a promotion and became a Development Worker.

In 2006, after much encouragement from my family, work colleagues, DOVE and DACE staff, I enrolled on the part-time degree programme at the Department of Adult Continuing Education (DACE), Swansea University. I was extremely nervous and doubted that I could ever achieve a degree. Although I worked in the centre where the South Wales Miners' Library has an outreach branch, I had no cause to ever use it, so my knowledge of what it provided was limited. On starting the degree it soon became apparent to me how integrally important the Miners' Library is in supporting students in their part-time study. Not only does it provide a vast array of books for your studies, but the help I received from Mandy, the library assistant who is based at DOVE one day a week, was over and above her job description.

Being an adult returning to study can be very daunting and studying from community venues makes it difficult to access materials and information from the main library on campus. However, the support, encouragement, help and the materials that I accessed from the Miners' Library, and also the book boxes they provided, has been integral to my achieving a BA Humanities honours degree. It is more than a library; it's a source of guidance, reassurance and a peaceful haven to study, particularly when you have three children at home. I still use the library on occasions and always feel relaxed when I return home. It's a wonderful asset to Swansea University, particularly to DACE students.

My experience of the South Wales Miners' Library has been one I am truly grateful for, without this magnificent resource and community centres like DOVE and Port Talbot YMCA, my end result of the part-time degree might have had a totally different outcome. I hope that many other students get to have the same experience as I have had; it has been truly life changing.

SIÂN TUCKER

'A LIFE-CHANGING EXPERIENCE'

Siân Tucker (right) talking to Susan Robeson
in July 2010. (Courtesy of Siân Williams)

The South Wales Miners' Library is very close to my heart and will always remain so as the part-time degree programme and the help and support of the Miners' Library changed my life.

With the encouragement and support of family and friends I enrolled on the part-time degree programme in 1999. However, having been confined to a wheelchair for a number of years I was very apprehensive about returning to study and lacked self-confidence and self-esteem. I needn't have worried as the whole experience changed my life and I loved every second of it. The South Wales Miners' Library in Hendrefoelan made borrowing books so easy and instilled in me a thirst for more and more knowledge and information and my passion for study took off. I achieved a first-class honours degree and received an award from the British Federation of Women Graduates, a dream come true. Further study with DACE followed and I graduated with a Masters in Lifelong Learning in 2009. I was delighted to become an associate lecturer with DACE and taught Social Policy at Banwen and had a real empathy with students as I knew exactly what they were going through.

Fortunately my health gradually improved and in 2007 I applied for a Community Archives Development Officer post as part of the Community Archives Wales project and I was delighted to be appointed to work in the South West Wales area. The highlight of this wonderful job was being based in the South Wales Miners' Library at Hendrefoelan House in one of the rooms overlooking the garden. It was a joy to walk up those stairs every morning to my office and I felt that all my Christmases had come at once. To work with Siân and the team was amazing and the two years I spent in post there will never be forgotten. Long may the South Wales Miners' Library continue to enrich lives.

Sir Deian Hopkin lectured on the role of libraries in the Digital Age at the South Wales Miners' Library on 16 October, 2012. (Courtesy of Siân Williams)

Opposite: The first leaflet produced for the South Wales Miners' Library in October 1973 stated that the Library 'is a living testimony to a generation of miners fervently committed to improving the standards of working class education'. The South Wales Miners' Library's present watchword is 'Preserving Your Past, Promoting Your Learning'.

THE NEW MILLENNIUM

At a Bevan Foundation lecture delivered at the South Wales Miners' Library in October 2012, Professor Sir Deian Hopkin, President of the National Library of Wales, spoke of the role libraries have to play in the Digital Age. He described how the old Miners' Institute and Welfare Hall libraries had their origins in educating those who could not afford to buy books. He argued that today, all libraries have a crucial role in providing access to and improving the education of everyone, particularly those from disadvantaged groups who may not have easy access to digital resources.

It was appropriate that this lecture should be given at the South Wales Miners' Library; the custodian of over sixty Miners' Institute and Welfare Hall Libraries, and the library which, for the past forty years, has endeavoured to maintain their traditions by breaking down barriers and being an inclusive resource, available to everyone.

The South Wales Miners' Library's work in preserving the research material amassed during the Coalfield History Projects of the early 1970s and 1980s has always been closely intertwined with the library's work in supporting Swansea University's widening access agenda through the Department of Adult Continuing Education (DACE) and its numerous innovative community based programmes which reach out to socially excluded groups. In the last twenty years, the South Wales Miners' Library has taken advantage of developments in technology, and opportunities to work in partnership with others, to provide online access to all the collections we hold and to enable their use in research, teaching and learning.

This chapter illustrates some of the highlights of the Library's work in the new millennium.

In 2006, the South Wales Miners' Library relocated a short distance from Hendrefoelan House to the Coach House building on Swansea University's Hendrefoelan campus. On 20 October 2006, at the opening ceremony, Tower Colliery Chairman, Tyrone O'Sullivan unveiled a painting entitled 'Three Miners on a Bench', which had been painted by the Ystradgynlais miner-artist, Cyril Ifold. (Courtesy of Swansea University)

LLAFUR
Welsh People's History Society
Cymdeithas Hanes Pobl Cymru

Day School on Welsh Political History
Ysgol Undydd Hanes Gwleidyddiaeth Cymru

Saturday 1 November 2003	*Dydd Sadwrn 1 Tachwedd 2003*
South Wales Miners' Library	*Llyfrgell Glowyr De Cymru*
Hendrefoelan House	*Tŷ Hendrefoelan*
University of Wales Swansea	*Prifysgol Cymru Abertawe*

Contributors to include / Cyfranwyr i gynnwys:

Professor K O Morgan	Wales in British Politics: Forty Years On
Dr Hywel Francis	Celebrating 30 years of the South Wales Miners' Library
Dr Nina Fishman	*Arthur Horner Memorial Lecture:* Solving the Enigma of Arthur Horner

Image courtesy of the South Wales Coalfield Collection, University of Wales Swansea

FREE *AM DDIM*
A warm welcome is extended to all *Croeso cynnes i bawb*

For further details please contact:
Am fanylion pellach cysylltwch â:

Steve Thompson
Adran Hanes a Hanes Cymru
UWA, Penglais, Aberystwyth, Ceredigion,
SY23 3DY
sdt@aber.ac.uk

Siân Williams
Librarian, South Wales Miners' Library
Hendrefoelan House, Gower Road, Swansea
SA2 7NB
s.f.williams@swan.ac.uk
Tel : 01792 518603/518693

The South Wales Miners' Library celebrated its thirtieth anniversary in October 2003 by hosting a Llafur event. K. O. Morgan, Hywel Francis and Nina Fishman all presented papers.

Staff outside the Library, September 2012. L–R: Martin Thomas, Caroline Crudge, Siân Williams, Mandy Orford, Joanne Waller, Rhian Phillips, Julie Came, Jill Hutchinson-Grigg.

Tyrone O'Sullivan, in the George Daggar Room at the South Wales Miners' Library, October 2006, with Siân Williams (left) and Hywel Francis (right). (Courtesy of Swansea University)

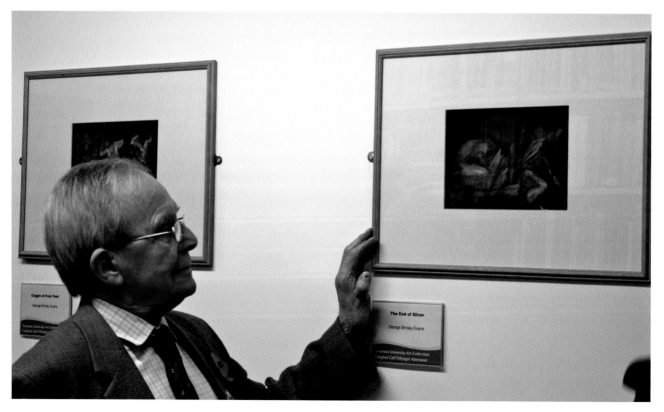

On his eighty-sixth birthday, on 8 November 2012, George Brinley Evans, a former miner and well known artist and author, presented two of his paintings to the South Wales Miners' Library. (Courtesy of Steve Williams)

The children from Ysgol Maes Y Coed in Bryncoch designed this banner as part of a Welsh Heritage Project on coalmining. We were delighted to display the banner in the South Wales Miners' Library during the summer of 2013.

In September 2011, a group of Clarion Cyclists called in to the South Wales Miners' Library as part of their tour of visiting Spanish Civil War memorials.

We are now able to accommodate IT classes and offer library and information skills sessions in our PC rooms.

(All images are courtesy of Siân Williams)

Distance And Lifelong Learning

The library services provided by the South Wales Miners' Library have always been designed to appreciate the difficulties students can face when juggling studies with other commitments, such as families, carer responsibilities, and work. The South Wales Miners' Library has historically adopted a four week loan and no fines policy: no fines are charged on the basis that finance should not be a barrier to education. We have operated a book box system since the early 1990s; a service which takes library books and resources into the community, directly to the students. These are unique services that the South Wales Miners' Library continues to offer to students in the Department of Adult Continuing Education today.

After 1997, new Government policies led to a marked increase in the number of part time students embarking on higher education. As a consequence, widening participation became a priority in higher education institutions across the country.

In response to the growing numbers of part time students studying a range of subjects at the University, the South Wales Miners' Library played a leading role in the development of a Swansea University library wide service aimed at part time and distance students, which for the first time allowed part time and distance students to request books to be sent to between branches of the University library service for collection, and provided a photocopy and postal service. In 2000, the service was renamed Distance And Lifelong Learners At Swansea, or DALLAS for short.

Other University libraries were also grappling with how to provide library support to the growing numbers of part time students embarking on courses, and so the DALLAS team organised and hosted a conference at Swansea University in April 2000. Over seventy librarians from around the UK attended to discuss the subject and witness the launch of the rebranded DALLAS service. Since then, the DALLAS service has evolved and accommodates online resources. However, the traditional book fetching service between the libraries is still at the heart of the service and is very well used.

The first DALLAS team comprised staff from Library & Information Services: (back, L–R) Rebecca Davies, Health Sciences Librarian; Sue Miller, Issue Desk Librarian; Madeleine Rogerson, Education Librarian, (front, L–R) Clare Boucher, Deputy Health Sciences Librarian; Siân Williams, Librarian, South Wales Miners' Library. (Courtesy of Swansea University)

COMMUNITY UNIVERSITY OF THE VALLEYS

The development of the Community University of the Valleys (CUV) at the DOVE Workshop in Banwen in 1992, a partnership between the Department of Adult Continuing Education (DACE) at Swansea University, DOVE Workshop and the Valleys Initiative for Adult Education, allowed students for the first time anywhere in the UK, to study for a degree in a community setting. The South Wales Miners' Library was an integral part of the CUV and established a branch library at Banwen.

The new millennium saw the scope of the CUV widen, both in terms of the range of courses that were available and the geographical spread. Other higher education institutions namely, the Open University in Wales, University of Glamorgan, and University of Wales College Newport, and twenty four community learning organisations throughout South Wales joined with the CUV to form the Community University of the Valleys Partnership.

Government and funding policies at this time placed increasing emphasis on widening participation and targeting previously under-represented groups. Higher education institutions had a key role to play in contributing to the regeneration and development of their local communities, and the CUV Partnership stakeholders aimed to work together, promoting the shared values of 'bringing learning closer to home', to develop appropriate lifelong learning opportunities for people in communities across West Wales and the Valleys, some of which were deemed to be in the most deprived areas of Wales.

Kenneth O. Morgan's opening words when he delivered the inaugural CUV lecture at Banwen in 1993 were,

> 'It is vital, for social and cultural as well as educational reasons, that the university remains in close touch with local grass-roots initiatives within the community'.

In 2003, during the tenth CUV Annual lecture, Jane Davidson, the then Education Minister in the Welsh Assembly Government, reiterated these words and then spoke of,

> 'the opportunities that advancing technology offers to the learning community ... we need not rely on individuals owning the technology. Community centres provide an important function in allowing adult learners to access PCs, the internet and other aids to learning – once again, a central role for the communities and community resources. These centres provide the support required and indeed, promote community learning in its purest sense'.

Jane Davidson AM, Minister for Education & Lifelong Learning giving the 10th Annual Community University of the Valleys Partnership Lecture at Onllwyn Miners' Welfare Hall on 19th November 2003 under banners from the collection at the South Wales Miners' Library. (Courtesy of Swansea University)

CONNECTING
COMMUNITIES CYMRU

In early 2000, the pioneering Connecting Communities Cymru project received funding from the European Regional Development Fund to install a suite of computers and a network link in two community centres in the valleys: the BELL Centre at Blaenllechau and the Bryncynon Community Development Centre. Two years earlier, the project, centred in DACE, had received funding to create computer suites in five community education centres in Community First areas. These were the Community Education Centre at Penlan, Swansea; the DOVE Workshop, Banwen; Glynneath Training Centre; Amman Valley Enterprise; and the Telecentre And Business School (TABS), Porth; and two teaching rooms on the main Swansea University campus. The project provided the infrastructure to deliver distance learning courses using the web, videoconferencing, video streaming, email and an ISDN link to the University library. The South Wales Miners' Library as a partner in

this project, worked closely with colleagues in DACE to explore new methods of delivering courses using this new technology. The first courses taught included 'Using the Internet for Music Resources', and 'Introduction to Sociology', which was taught by video conference: the tutor was in Swansea and the students in Glynneath.

South Wales Miners' Library staff visited the centres, providing traditional face to face information and IT skills sessions, as of course the students needed to know how to use the equipment. It became apparent that a more structured IT literacy course was needed, and so South Wales Miners' Library staff, Clare Boucher and Siân Williams developed a ten week course called Navigating the Information Maze. Clare and Siân taught a pilot course at Glynneath Training Centre. Due to its success, Siân then taught it at again at Glynneath and at the DOVE Workshop, Banwen.

As the students' confidence at using this technology increased, so did ours and as part of the Technology, Research and Innovation project (TRIO), with assistance from the project staff, we developed an online version

Students on the Introduction to Sociology course at Glynneath Training Centre. Their tutor can be seen on the computer screen on the left. The course was taught by video conference from the Swansea University campus. (Courtesy of Swansea University)

of the Navigating the Information Maze course. The TRIO project based in DACE between 2006 and 2008, encouraged people working in small and medium sized enterprises (SMEs), Community Enterprises and the Voluntary Sector to study online for a Higher Education Certificate. Students learnt about and used the latest social media technologies including blogs and podcasts.

The aim of the TRIO project was to design and create an online learning environment in which students could come together to learn and share their ideas. It endeavoured to create more than just a virtual learning environment (VLE) which was used by tutors and students as a place to store and access documents; it was pioneering in that it wanted to create an online environment that would encourage students to interact with their tutors and peers online and take control of their learning.

In recent years there has been a growth in online higher education courses. The provision of these types of courses, such as MOOCs (Massive Open Online Courses), is a current topic of discussion in Wales, with the Welsh Government Minister for Education and Skills, establishing an Online Digital Learning Resources Working Group in February 2013.

Opening the Library to the World

Although these projects, including the Community University of the Valleys Partnership, have come to an end, the South Wales Miners' Library carries forward their legacies in many new ways.

Addressing the digital divide and providing access to our library services to everyone, especially those from disadvantaged groups, is challenging. DACE teach a range of courses from the Pathways and taster

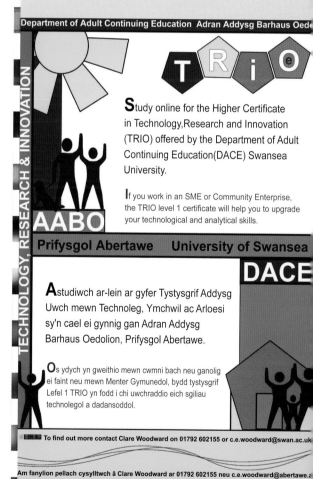

Department of Adult Continuing Education Adran Addysg Barhaus Oede

Study online for the Higher Certificate in Technology, Research and Innovation (TRIO) offered by the Department of Adult Continuing Education(DACE) Swansea University.

If you work in an SME or Community Enterprise, the TRIO level 1 certificate will help you to upgrade your technological and analytical skills.

Prifysgol Abertawe   University of Swansea

DACE

Astudiwch ar-lein ar gyfer Tystysgrif Addysg Uwch mewn Technoleg, Ymchwil ac Arloesi sy'n cael ei gynnig gan Adran Addysg Barhaus Oedolion, Prifysgol Abertawe.

Os ydych yn gweithio mewn cwmni bach neu ganolig ei faint neu mewn Menter Gymunedol, bydd tystysgrif Lefel 1 TRIO yn fodd i chi uwchraddio eich sgiliau technolegol a dadansoddol.

To find out more contact Clare Woodward on 01792 602155 or c.e.woodward@swan.ac.uk

Am fanylion pellach cysylltwch â Clare Woodward ar 01792 602155 neu c.e.woodward@abertawe.a

courses, which are short courses with no formal assessment, to the Accredited programme, which allows students to work towards a Higher Education Certificate or Diploma to the Part Time Degree programme. With the majority of pathways and accredited courses being taught in community locations, and the part time degree now being taught in fourteen venues in the counties of Swansea, Neath Port Talbot, Carmarthenshire and Pembrokeshire, the South Wales Miners' Library has had to adapt and be creative in the way in which we support the students, particularly those living and studying at a distance.

The advances in technology have not just impacted on the educational role of the South Wales Miners' Library. Until the mid 1990s, researchers and students had to contact South Wales Miners' Library staff or visit the Library to determine what was held in its research collections. Making use of the developing technologies, the first online catalogue for the South Wales Coalfield Collection appeared in 1995 as a result of funding from the Higher Education Funding Council for Wales (HEFCW).

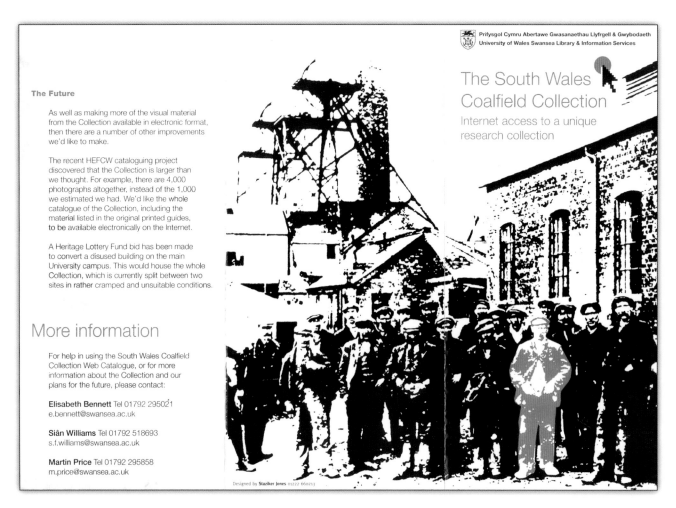

The material collected as part of the Coalfield History projects was renamed the South Wales Coalfield Collection in 1995. The collection is divided between the South Wales Miners' Library and the University Archives (now known as the Richard Burton Archives).

Pictured at the first meeting of the South Wales Coalfield Collection Development Committee in 2004 are: (L–R) Sara Marsh, Deputy Director of Library & Information Services; Jane Elliott, Deputy Director of the Department of Adult Continuing Education; Siân Williams; Chris West, Director of Library & Information Services; Elisabeth Bennett; Wayne Thomas, Secretary, South Wales Area NUM; Nina Fishman, History Department, Swansea University; Louise Miskell, History Department, Swansea University; Dr Hywel Francis MP, Chair of the Committee. (Courtesy of Swansea University)

Coalfield Web Materials Project Manager Alex Roberts, Dr Hywel Francis MP, Prof Sir Glanmor Williams, Mine of Information Project Manager Adam Green, and Prof W. A. Cole at an event in July 2002 to highlight the work of the two projects in increasing access to the South Wales Coalfield Collection. Professor Williams and Professor Cole were the joint project directors of the SSRC project which set up the South Wales Miners' Library in 1973. (Courtesy of Swansea University)

Website tunnels way in to mining history

By Jonathan Isaacs

UNIQUE RECORD Alex Roberts, project manager of the web-based museum for South Wales Coalfields (centre), with (from left) university archivist Elizabeth Bennet, South Wales Miners Library senior library assistant Jo Waller, librarian Sian Williams, project assistant Wendy Sheridan, project archivist Julie Anderson and video editor Justine Dolan.

The Coalfield Web Materials Project staff (Courtesy of the *South Wales Evening Post*).

THE history of the South Wales coalfield is one of the richest of any industry in the world.

Coal mining in South Wales was at the centre of Britain's economic and political life for most of the 20th Century.

From the general strike of 1926, the hunger marches of the late 1920s and early 1930s, the nationalisation of Britain's coal industry in 1947 to the last desperate strike of 1984-5, South Wales miners always led from the front.

A huge amount of that rich tapestry has been recorded by the University of Wales's South Wales Coalfield Collection based in Swansea.

Now, thanks to funding from the New Opportunities Fund, it has been transposed on to a new Swansea University website, Coalfield Web Materials, or Cwm for short.

Project manager Alex Roberts said it provided a unique record of the history of the South Wales coalfield.

"We have digitised photographic and oral history contained in the coalfield collection, both in audio and video form," said Alex.

"There are interviews with miners' leaders, politicians, and ordinary miners to give a unique record of life in the coalfield of the last century."

The interviews are invaluable for they will ensure the personal stories of the people who lived through the events are kept for posterity.

Themes include the impact of the coal industry on the valleys and political issues, including the rise of the Labour Party.

The website, the only one of its type in the world, looks at religion, education, leisure, culture and family life in the South Wales mining communities through the eyes of the people with first-hand experience.

Users will be able to tune in and listen to interviews with key players in the coalfield over 100 years leading up to the 1984-5 miners' strike.

"Our mission is to improve lifelong learning opportunities by stimulating and maintaining interest in the local history and cultural heritage of South Wales," said Alex.

The website is backed by nearly a century of pictures of the pits and valley life in South Wales, the hunger marches, the protests and picket lines.

● **The website can be accessed at www.agor.org.uk**

The catalogue included the oral history, video and banner collections held at the South Wales Miners' Library and the photograph and the manuscript collections held in the University Archives. For the first time, people could search the collections using any PC with an internet connection. This development saw a dramatic increase in the number of enquiries the South Wales Miners' Library received, particularly from abroad.

The Mine of Information project, launched in 2000 with funds from the Research Support Libraries Programme, aimed to assist us further to improve access to research collections held at the South Wales Miners' Library and University Archives. A Librarian, Rachael Whitfield, and two Archivists, Helen Briscoe and Kate Mason, were appointed to create computer catalogue records. Rachael was based at the South Wales Miners' Library and catalogued our extensive pamphlet collections, while Kate and Helen catalogued a number of collections in the Archives. This ambitious project saw us working in partnership with other universities and record offices, with the aim of creating a web based catalogue which contained the newly created records from our collections and the records of similar material about the South Wales coalfield held in the partner collections.

The project paved the way for the Coalfield Web Materials Project. Funded by the New Opportunities Fund in 2002, it allowed the South Wales Miners' Library to digitise oral history material (in both audio and video format) and the Richard Burton Archives to digitise photographs and make them available via the internet. There was an educational aspect to this project, and we worked with an educational consultant to ensure the resulting website provided learning opportunities for all by stimulating interest in the local history and cultural heritage of South Wales.

Since then, the South Wales Miners' Library, along with the Richard Burton Archives, has striven to keep abreast with technological developments and opportunities to promote their research collections to the wider community. Working in partnership with other libraries and archives, the South Wales Miners' Library and Richard Burton Archives have been able to digitise parts of our collections. For example, material relating to the First World War has been digitised and will form part of a Wales wide project 'The Welsh Experience of World War One' to mark the centenary of the Great War in 2014.

A Wellcome Trust grant in 2004, enabled the South Wales Miners' Library and the Richard Burton Archives to work in partnership with Swansea University's Department of Health Sciences to undertake a project called *Identifying Medical Records in the South Wales Coalfield Collection*. Focusing on community and occupation health, Dr Sara Brady and Professor Anne Borsay trawled through the collections to locate and document the often hidden records which could assist – and identify – future research in this field, and highlight the medical and healthcare heritage of the South Wales Coalfield. The resulting publication *Medical Records for the South Wales Coalfield: An Annotated Guide to the South Wales Coalfield Collection*, and the online catalogue accessible via the Coalfield Web Materials website has paved the way for more research in this area.

The South Wales Miners' Library is pleased to be supporting the five year Disability and Industrial Society project, which is funded by the Wellcome Trust. This collaborative and comparative project runs until 2016, and will explore how the experiences of disability were affected by industrialisation between 1780 and 1948. The project focuses on the coal industry, and will compare the coalfields in south Wales, north east England and central Scotland.

Using the collections to promote education and skills to socially excluded groups has always been a priority. We were delighted therefore in 2007 to have the opportunity to participate in a two year project, led by Culturenet Cymru at the National Library of Wales, which encouraged people living in Communities First areas to develop the skills to record their own

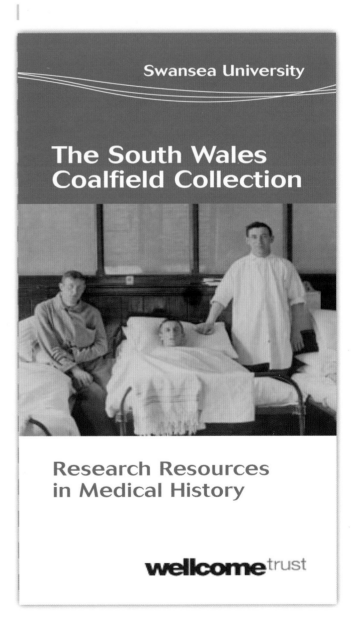

Swansea University

The South Wales Coalfield Collection

Research Resources in Medical History

wellcometrust

community history in a digital format. Indeed, Siân Tucker, one of the Project Officers on the Community Archives Wales project was based at the South Wales Miners' Library for the duration of the project. The project team, funded by Communities@One, an initiative of the Communities First programme in Wales, worked with eleven community groups in some of the most deprived areas of Wales. The participants in the project were shown the skills to digitise their photographs and create their own digital community archives and share them on the Community Archives Wales website. The community group members were encouraged to work with other community groups who were not formally part of the project and teach them their newly acquired skills.

The Community Archives Wales project website : http://www.ourwales.org.uk/.

BRINGING THE LIBRARY TO THE PEOPLE

The South Wales Miners' Library in the new millennium has played a leading role with its many partners, including the Welsh Government, in mounting major educational exhibitions.

Above: (L-R) Siân Williams and Huw Lewis AM, then Minister for Housing, Regeneration & Heritage. Huw Lewis visited the South Wales Miners' Library on 8 December 2011. (Courtesy of Mandy Orford)

LEST WE FORGET: UNFURLING THE SOUTH WALES MINERS' BANNERS COLLECTION

The banner collection evokes strong emotions from people living in former mining communities. Having become too fragile to march behind and even display, in 2004, the Heritage Lottery Fund awarded the South Wales Miners' Library a grant to conserve five of the most damaged banners, provide better storage conditions, create replicas of the NUM banners and produce an exhibition about South Wales miners' banners, with accompanying educational resources. The exhibition has toured many schools, museums and festivals throughout the country.

Marching Forward!
An exhibition of
Welsh banners

In 2005, with a grant from the Welsh Government, Siân Williams curated an exhibition at Newport Museum & Art Gallery, which considered the social history of Wales through the banners which had been used in parades, marches and protests all over the country. The earliest of the thirty banners on display, a Friendly Society banner from Radnorshire, dated from the mid 1800s. Other banners in the exhibition were from trade unions, temperance groups, co-operative societies, suffragettes, peace groups and political parties.

Marching Forward! Exhibition programme.

The exhibition at Newtown Library.
(Courtesy of The Co-operative Cymru/ Wales)

ROBERT OWEN: LEGACIES THAT LAST

Working in partnership with the Co-operative Group and the Robert Owen Network, the South Wales Miners' Library developed a bilingual exhibition to mark the 150th anniversary of the death of Robert Owen, the 'father' of the Co-operative Movement. Launched at the Senedd in Cardiff in February 2008, the exhibition was displayed in a variety of venues throughout the UK from academic conferences, libraries and museums to co-op shops, so as to reach as wide and diverse an audience as possible. With grants from the Welsh Government and the Heritage Lottery Fund, educational resources were also produced which could be used by teachers and community groups.

Paul Robeson Jr presents the 'Let Paul Robeson Sing!' exhibition to the South Wales Miners' Library in October 2007. (Courtesy of Swansea University)

LET PAUL ROBESON SING!

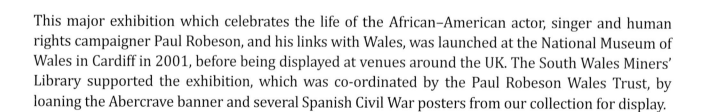

This major exhibition which celebrates the life of the African–American actor, singer and human rights campaigner Paul Robeson, and his links with Wales, was launched at the National Museum of Wales in Cardiff in 2001, before being displayed at venues around the UK. The South Wales Miners' Library supported the exhibition, which was co-ordinated by the Paul Robeson Wales Trust, by loaning the Abercrave banner and several Spanish Civil War posters from our collection for display.

Paul Robeson first came into contact with a group of South Wales miners in the 1920s. He maintained links with the South Wales Miners' Federation and its successor the South Wales Area of the National Union of Mineworkers for the rest of his life. After he died in 1976, his son Paul Robeson Jr continued the relationship with South Wales and visited the South Wales Miners' Library in 1989. Paul Robeson Jr and his wife Marilyn visited again in October 2007, when fifty years after the secretly arranged transatlantic broadcast from a New York studio to the Miners' Eisteddford in Porthcawl, Paul Jr presided over the ceremony which placed the 'Let Paul Robeson Sing!' exhibition into the care of the South Wales Miners' Library.

Three years later, at the National Eisteddfod at Ebbw Vale in August 2010, Alun Ffred Jones, the then Heritage Minister in Welsh Assembly Government, launched a bilingual online learning resource based on the 'Let Paul Robeson Sing!' exhibition, which had been developed by the South Wales Miners' Library.

The resource was created with the financial support of the Welsh Assembly Government to form part of the online People's Collection Wales, an initiative which was also being launched at the National Eisteddfod. (http://www.peoplescollectionwales.co.uk/)

Also present at the launch was Susan Robeson, the grand-daughter of Paul. With the support of the Welsh Assembly Government and the Paul Robeson Wales Trust, the South Wales Miners' Library was able to host Susan Robeson's first visit to Wales. The last time the National Eisteddfod had been held at Ebbw Vale (in 1958), Paul Robeson had attended, where he spoke of his love for Wales and its people, saying 'You have shaped my life – I have learned from you'.

Fifty two years later, the warm welcome Susan received at the 2010 National Eisteddfod showed how much affection there is still for her grandfather. During her three week visit, Susan gave lectures and led workshops for children about her grandfather and his legacy.

Susan being interviewed for BBC Radio Wales at the National Eisteddfod, Ebbw Vale in 2010.

Left: Susan with children who attended her workshop at the National Waterfront Museum in Swansea.

All images are courtesy of Siân Williams

JOHN FROST

In July 2013, the South Wales Miners' Library loaned a framed photograph of Welsh Chartist leader, John Frost to the House of Commons for inclusion in an exhibition to mark the 175th anniversary of The People's Charter. The exhibition was opened by Mr Speaker Bercow.

In 1974, the framed photograph was donated to the South Wales Miners' Library by Edgar Evans of Bedlinog. During an oral history interview in July 1973, Edgar Evans revealed the photograph had belonged to Joe Sparkes, the great-grandnephew of John Frost. He explained that Joe Sparkes himself 'was an extraordinary character'. He had worked as a collier, but after being victimised, had moved to Bedlinog where he began selling meat by 'going round house to house with a basket on his arm'. He eventually opened a grocery shop in Bedlinog, but always retained 'his militancy and his views'.

Above and left: The photograph was displayed in the exhibition in Parliament during the summer of 2013. All photos are courtesy of Simon O'Connor and the Archives & Records Association.

Opposite: In November 1839, four thousand Chartists, mostly miners, converged on Newport. They were led by John Frost. In response, the authorities held the Chartist leaders in the Westgate Hotel. As the protestors besieged the hotel and chanted for the release of the prisoners, soldiers fired into the crowd, killing fourteen people and wounding over fifty. The Chartist leaders, John Frost, Zephaniah Williams and William Jones, were charged as traitors and sentenced to death. They were later reprieved and transported to Tasmania.

Above: On 8 December 1973, less than two months after the South Wales Miners' Library opened, the *South Wales Evening Post* reported on a visit of three Russian poets and writers to the Library. (Courtesy of the *South Wales Evening Post*)

Left: The South Wales miners who visited the Appalachian Coalfields in May 1979 beneath the portrait portrait of the US miners' leader John L. Lewis. (Courtesy of Hywel Francis)

INTERNATIONAL LINKS

The South Wales Miners' Library has attracted the attention of people from all over the world. Since its opening in 1973, the library has welcomed visitors from France, Germany, Spain, Ireland, as well as Japan, Australia and the USA.

The South Wales Miners' Library has long established links with the Appalachian Coalfields in the USA. In 1976, Professor Helen Lewis of the University of Virginia was based for six months in the Library for her comparative study of American and South Wales miners. John Gaventa, a political sociologist and Richard Greatrex, a photographer and film maker, worked with Helen to record the experiences of people living in the Amman Valley.

The study did not just focus on the miners, but the community as a whole. One interview for example, was held with a group of young women who lived in Brynamman. They talked about their families, the lack of work for women in the area, and how their standard of living compared with that of their parents. They spoke of the sense of community in Brynamman and how women in mining communities differed from other women. They also shared their thoughts on the dangers of mining and the possibility of their husbands being killed.

Similar interviews were conducted by Helen Lewis and her colleagues in Appalachia. This comparative research has been built upon over the years, and included a visit by a group of Welsh miners to Appalachia in 1979.

Since 2001, groups of Appalachian State University students have visited the Dulais and Afan Valleys on field trips every few years, using the research resources at the South Wales Miners' Library and Banwen Library.

The social, economic and environmental changes in the last forty years in South Wales and Appalachia have been similar. The coalfield is in decline in Appalachia, while there are very few jobs in the coal industry in South Wales. Building on the comparative work conducted over the last forty years, in June 2013, Dr Patricia Beaver and Tom Hansell of Appalachia State University, gave a showing of their documentary 'After Coal: Welsh and Appalachian Mining Communities' at the DOVE Workshop in Banwen and at the South Wales Miners' Museum.

SOUTH WALES MINERS IN AMERICA

Report of the first Rank and File
British Miners' Delegation to visit
the United States Coalfields,

MAY, 1979

Published by

BRYNLLIW and MARDY LODGES
of the N.U.M.

Edited by

HYWEL FRANCIS
South Wales Miners' Library,
Department of Extra-Mural Studies,
University College of Swansea.

The Smithsonian Folklife Festival is an annual, cultural festival which takes places outdoors on the National Mall in Washington, DC. In 2009, Wales was the featured nation of the two week festival. Siân Williams was invited to take part and organised a display which included material from the South Wales Miners' Library collection, including pamphlets, illustrations, posters, oral history extracts and banners to represent the history and legacy of the Welsh coal industry. Wayne Thomas, the Secretary of the South Wales Area of the National Union of Mineworkers also attended, and between them, they welcomed thousands of visitors to their stand.

All images are courtesy of Siân Williams.

SPA & INN
THE MAPLE LODGE

日本とウェールズにおける炭鉱の記憶
Collective Memories of Coal Mining in Japan and Wales

地域再生へのアーカイブズと社会教育の役割　The Roles of Archives and Social Education towards Community Regeneration

●主催● 旧産炭地研究会（JAFCOF）、NPO法人炭鉱の記憶推進事業団、早稲田大学ライフコースアーカイブ研究所

●後援● 北海道空知支庁、岩見沢市、美唄市、札幌学院大学、スウォンジー大学、日本学術振興会、英国学士院、大和日英基金、北海道産業考古学会、NPO法人北海道遺産協議会

Group photo taken during the second visit to Hokkaido, Japan in August 2009. (Courtesy of Siân Williams)

A chance visit from a Japanese academic to the South Wales Miners' Library and the Richard Burton Archives in 2007, formed the basis of a three year project between Swansea University and academics in Japan to compare the history and regeneration of the coalfields in Wales and Japan.

Professor Chris Williams from the History Department, Jane Elliott from DACE, Elisabeth Bennett from the RBA and Siân Williams from the South Wales Miners' Library formed Swansea University's delegation and visited the Japanese coalfields in Hokkaido and Joban. On return visits, we took our Japanese colleagues on a tour of the South Wales and North Wales coalfields.

At the symposia organised in Japan and Wales, we took part in presentations and discussions on the decline of coal mining in South Wales and Japan; the regeneration strategies implemented; an assessment of the role of educational initiatives in regeneration; the importance of historical understanding to the collective memory

Construction at the site of Swansea University's Science and Innovation Bay Campus in October 2013, looking northwards towards the mountains and valleys beyond Neath and Port Talbot. (Courtesy of Swansea University)

of the coalfield society; and the role of archives, libraries and museums in regeneration. We also provided practical support and advice in the care and development of archives and special collections to our Japanese colleagues.

We hope that the example provided by the South Wales Miners' Library in its first four decades through its unique democratic combination of scholarship, widening access and partnership with local and international communities will be an inspiration for Swansea University in shaping the new millennium, inspired by the eternal belief that knowledge – in its economic, cultural and democratic forms – truly is power.

The South Wales Miners' Library – and the workmen's institute libraries before it – has striven to create not just a knowledge economy but, more importantly, a knowledge society. What better aspiration could Swansea University have for this new millennium, with the opportunities afforded by its new Science and Innovation Campus.

Oral History Interviews Referred to in the Text

Interviewee	Interviewer(s)	Date of interview	Reference
Archie Lush	Hywel Francis	11 May 1973	AUD/ 338
Will Paynter	Hywel Francis & David Smith	18 April 1969	AUD/446
Abel Morgan	David Egan & Merfyn Jones	9 October 1972	AUD/311
J. L. Williams	David Egan	24 April 1973	AUD/396
William Knipe	David Egan	2 February 1973	AUD/344
Tom Watkins	David Egan	23 October 1972	AUD/335
William Rosser Jones	Hywel Francis	4 July 1973	AUD/180
Dai Dan Evans	Hywel Francis	5 December 1972	AUD/263
Will Arthur	David Egan & Merfyn Jones	21 May 1973	AUD/317
D. J. Davies	David Egan	3 November 1972	AUD/173
Ben Davies	Hywel Francis	11 June 1973	AUD/168
Max Goldberg	Hywel Francis	6 September 1972	AUD/347
Merfyn Payne	Hywel Francis	18 June 1975	AUD/395
Glyn Williams	Alun Morgan	20 March 1973	AUD/258
Elvet Evans	Alun Burge	1978	AUD/621
Reg Fine	Hywel Francis	2 July 1973	AUD/184
Will 'Post' Rees	Hywel Francis	26 April 1974	AUD/259
Mavis Llewellyn	Hywel Francis	20 May 1974	AUD/98
Maria Williams	Hywel Francis	1 July 1973	AUD/183
Jim Brewer	Hywel Francis	29 November 1969	AUD/2
Rosa Steel	SWML staff	1985	VID/32
Dai Francis	David Smith	21 June 1976	AUD/ 452
O. Edwards	Alun Morgan	2 November 1973	AUD/217
Dane Hartwell	Kim Howells	18 March 1980	AUD/125
Alec Jones	Kim Howells	17 January 1980	AUD/59
Neil Kinnock	Kim Howells	1980	AUD/30
Cwm Llantwit Women's Support Group	WCCPL	2 August 1984	AUD/584
Maerdy Women's Support Group	WCCPL	2 August 1984	AUD/585

Details of all the interviews held at the South Wales Miners' Library can be found on our catalogue at www. agor.org.uk/cwm. Visitors are welcome to visit the South Wales Miners' Library to listen to or view the interviews and consult accompanying transcripts where they exist.

Select Bibliography

Elizabeth Andrews, *A Woman's Work is Never Done*, Honno, 2006.

Chris Baggs, *The Miners' Libraries of South Wales from the 1860s to 1939*, unpublished Ph.D., University of Wales Aberystwyth, 1995.

Chris Baggs, '"Well done Cymmer Workmen!", The Cymmer Collieries Workmen's Library', 1893-1920, *Llafur, vol. 5*, no. 3, 1990.

Deirdre Beddoe, *Out of the Shadows: A History of Women in Twentieth Century Wales*, University of Wales Press, 2001.

Aneurin Bevan, *In Place of Fear*, Heinemann, 1952, reprinted Quartet, 1990.

Anne Borsay & Sara Knight, *Medical Records for the South Wales Coalfield, c.1890-1948: An Annotated Guide to the South Wales Coalfield Collection*, University of Wales Press, 2007.

Sue Bruley, *The Women and Men of 1926: A Gender and Social History of the General Strike and Miners' Lockout in South Wales*, University of Wales Press, 2010.

Alun Burge, "Miners Learning in the South Wales Coalfield 1900-1947", *Llafur, vol. 8*, no. 1, 2000.

Alun Burge, 'The Co-operative Movement in South Wales and its History: "a task worthy of the most sincere devotion and application"', *Welsh History Review, vol. 23*, no. 4, 2007.

Ben Curtis, *The South Wales Miners 1964-1985*, University of Wales Press, 2013.

D.J. Davies, *Ninety Years of Endeavour: Tredegar Workmen's Hall, 1861-1951*, Western Mail and Echo, 1951.

Keith Davies, '"A healthier and profitable choice": the Carnegie Trust and adult education in the South Wales coalfield in the early 1930s', *History of Education Society Bulletin*, No 63, May 1999.

Keith Davies & Alun Burge, 'Enlightenment of the highest order: the education programme of the South Wales miners 1956-1971', *Llafur, vol. 7*, no 1, 1996.

David L. Davies, *A History of Cwmaman Institute*, D. J. Pryce and Sons, 1982.

David Egan, *Coal Society: A History of the South Wales Mining Valleys 1840-1980*, Gomer, 1987.

David Egan, 'The Unofficial Reform Committee and the Miners' Next Step', *Llafur, vol. 2*, no. 3, 1978.

Jane Elliott, Hywel Francis, Rob Humphreys & David Istance, *Communities and their Universities: The Challenge of Lifelong Learning*, Lawrence and Wishart, 1996.

Michael Foot, *Aneurin Bevan: A Biography, vol. 1*: 1897-1945, MacGibbon and Kee, 1962, reprinted Faber & Faber, 2008.

Michael Foot, *Aneurin Bevan: A Biography, vol. 2*: 1945-1960, Davis-Poynter, 1973, reprinted Faber & Faber, 2008.

Hywel Francis, 'Do Miners Read Dickens? Communities, Universities and a New Beginning', *Welsh Journal of Education, vol. 6*, no. 1, 1997.

Hywel Francis, *History On Our Side: Wales and the 1984/5 Miners' Strike*, Iconau, 2009.

Hywel Francis, 'Intellectual Property, First Time Round: the Re-invention of the South Wales Miners' Library', *Llafur, vol. 9*, no. 1, 2004.

Hywel Francis, *Miners Against Fascism: Wales and the Spanish Civil War*, Lawrence & Wishart, 1984, reprinted Lawrence and Wishart, 2012.

Hywel Francis, 'Origins of the South Wales Miners' Library', *History Workshop Journal*, no 2, Autumn 1976.

Hywel Francis, 'Survey of Workmen's Institute and Welfare Hall Libraries', *Llafur, vol. 1*, no. 2, 1973.

Hywel Francis & Dai Smith, *The Fed: A history of the South Wales Miners in the Twentieth Century*, Lawrence and Wishart, 1980, reprinted University of Wales Press, 1998.

Mair Francis, *Up the DOVE: The History of the DOVE Workshop in Banwen*, Iconau, 2008.

Menna Gallie, *The Small Mine*, Gollancz, 1962.

George H. Hoare, *The History of the Oakdale Institute 1912-1946*, Newport, 1950.

Angela John, 'A Miner Struggle? Women's protest in Welsh mining history', *Llafur, vol. 4*, no. 1, 1984.

Angela John ed, *Our Mother's Land: Chapters in Welsh Women's History 1830-1939*, University of Wales Press, 1991, reprinted University of Wales Press, 2011.

Thomas Jones, *Leeks and Daffodils*, Welsh Outlook Press, 1942.

Daryl Leeworthy, *Workers' Fields: Sport, Landscape and the Labour Movement in South Wales, 1858–1958*, unpublished Ph.D., Swansea University, 2011.

Richard Lewis, *Leaders and Teachers: Adult Education and the Challenge of Labour in South Wales 1906-1940*, University of Wales Press, 1993.

Gerallt D. Nash, T. A. Davies & Beth Thomas, *Workmen's Halls and Institutes: Oakdale Workmen's Institute*, National Museums and Galleries of Wales, 1995.

John Roe, *The Public Library in Wales: Its History and Development in the Context of Local Government*, unpublished M.A., Queen's University of Belfast, 1970.

Jonathan Rose, *The Intellectual Life of the British Working Classes*, Yale University Press, 2001.

Dai Smith, *Aneurin Bevan and the World of South Wales*, University of Wales Press, 1993.

Dai Smith, *In the Frame: Wales in Society 1910-2010*, Parthian, 2010.

Dai Smith, *Raymond Williams: A Warrior's Tale*, Parthian, 2007.

Peter Stead, *Coleg Harlech: The First Fifty Years*, University of Wales Press, 1977.

Colin Trotman & Hywel Francis, 'A Continuity of Purpose? Education and the South Wales miners', in Anthony Cooke and Ann MacSween, eds, *The Rise and Fall of Adult Institutions and Social Movements: The Proceedings of the Seventh International Conference on the History of Adult Education*, Peter Lang, 2000.

Colin Trotman et al. *Transformation, Progression and Hope: Whatever Happened to Lifelong Learning?*, Forum for Access and Continuing Education, 2007.

Chris Williams, Capitalism, *Community and Conflict: the South Wales Coalfield 1898-1947*, University of Wales Press, 1993.

Chris Williams, *Democratic Rhondda: Politics and Society 1885-1951*, University of Wales Press, 1996.

ACKNOWLEDGMENTS

In writing this account of the first forty years of the South Wales Miners' Library, we have been helped by a wide range of people. We are grateful to Swansea University's Vice Chancellor Richard Davies, and Pro-Vice Chancellors Professor Iwan Davies and Professor Noel Thompson for their support. Kevin Daniel and Steve Williams, Director and Deputy Director of Information Services and Systems at Swansea University have also been very generous in their support and encouragement.

We of course acknowledge the major roles of David Egan, Merfyn Jones, Alun Morgan, Connie Jones and Mona Robinson who worked on the first SSRC funded South Wales Coalfield History Project and Kim Howells and Lynda Willmott, who worked on the second project between 1979 and 1982. The vision of the late Professor Glanmor Williams and Professor Alan (Max) Cole, Directors of the first project, must also be recorded with appreciation. We also thank Nan Campbell and Nicola Stonelake for their sterling work in the Library.

We wish to thank our friends and colleagues who have contributed to the publication of this book in many different ways. In particular, we wish to thank Alun Burge, George Brinley Evans, Richard Greatrex, Denise Lewis, Mandy Orford, Tyrone O'Sullivan, Colin Trotman, Siân Tucker, and Chris Williams for sharing their reminiscences of the Library so willingly. Our friend Alun Burge has been especially helpful in proof reading and advising on the book, as has Jaselle Williams.

The current staff at the South Wales Miners' Library: Julie Came, Caroline Crudge, Jill Hutchinson-Grigg, Mandy Orford, Martin Thomas, Rhian Phillips, and Joanne Waller have gone beyond the call of duty in their help and support.

We are grateful to Elisabeth Bennett and Sue Thomas of the Richard Burton Archives, Swansea University and Cathy Duncan and Pat Jones of the *South Wales Evening Post* for their assistance. We wish to thank Steve Howell, Susan Robeson, Steve Williams, David Yendoll, the Co-operative Cymru/Wales, the Wales Council for Voluntary Action, *The Times* and the National Coal Mining Museum for England for granting us permission to use their photographs. We also thank Bryn Griffiths for kindly allowing us to reproduce verses from his poem 'The Death of Duffryn Rhondda'.

We thank Wayne Thomas of the National Union of Mineworkers (South Wales Area) who has been unstinting in his enthusiastic support of the South Wales Miners' Library, as have many of his members over many decades.

Our biggest debt is to our families and in particular to Mair and Paul who have over the years endured our enthusiasms and tolerated our obsessions.

Finally, we wish to thank Richard Davies, Claire Houguez, Kate Ellis and Robert Harries of Parthian Books for their professionalism and encouragement in making this book possible. All errors are our own.

Contributors

Hywel Francis is the founder of the South Wales Miners' Library, where he was an organiser of miners' day-release and residential courses (1975-89). He was Professor of Continuing Education at Swansea University until he became Labour MP for Aberavon in 2001. He is chair of the Joint Committee on Human Rights and the All Party Parliamentary Group on Archives and History, and an Emeritus Professor at Swansea University.

Siân Williams has been the Librarian of the South Wales Miners' Library since 1995. A qualified Librarian, she is a member of the Wales Higher Education Libraries Forum (WHELF) Archives and Special Collections Group; Chair of the Wales Audio–Visual Archives Forum; a Trustee of the Paul Robeson Wales Trust; and Secretary of Llafur: the Welsh People's History Society.

Alun Burge has worked with co-operatives since 1985 in a variety of national and international roles and is currently a member of the Advisory Group supporting the Welsh Government's Co-operatives and Mutuals Commission in Wales. He is a long-standing member of Llafur, and is a frequent contributor to the journal. He is writing a volume on *William Hazell and the Gleaming Vision for the South Wales Records Society* and is also working on a history of the Wales Co-operative Centre.

George Brinley Evans was born in Dyffryn Cellwen in 1925. Aged fourteen, he began working in the Banwen Colliery in 1939 and then served in Burma with the 12th Army during the Second World War. He returned to the mines after the war and began working in open cast mining in 1977. During his working life he became an established painter and despite losing an eye in an accident, also began to develop as a sculptor and writer. His paintings and sculptures have been widely exhibited. He published his first book, *Boys of Gold* (Parthian, 2000), at the age of seventy-seven.

Richard Greatrex was brought up in Swansea where he trained as an electrician. In 1970 he found higher education and in 1974 John Gaventa found him. With him he discovered film making and spent thirty years as a Director of Photography. In 1998, he received a BAFTA Award for *The Woman in White*, and in 1999 received an Oscar nomination for his work on *Shakespeare in Love*. He retired in 2010 and rediscovered photography. In 2013, he re-found the South Wales Miners' Library.

Denise Lewis is from Crynant in the Dulais Valley. She has worked as a Community Development Worker for the Cwmdulais Uchaf Communities First Team based at DOVE Workshop, Banwen for over ten years. After leaving school without any qualifications, Denise enrolled on the part-time BA Humanities degree at Swansea University, and graduated with a first-class honours degree in 2012.

Rhodri Morgan was appointed as Chancellor of Swansea University in 2011. He was Labour MP for Cardiff West from 1987 until he stood down at the 2001 General Election, having been elected as AM for Cardiff West in 1999. He was appointed First Secretary of Wales in 2000, a title which later became First Minister for Wales and which he held until he retired in 2009.

Robert Morgan was a Cynon Valley miner who later trained as a teacher. His poetry was published widely and his paintings were also exhibited. He died in 1994.

MANDY ORFORD attended several courses at the DOVE Workshop before being appointed as a Library Assistant at the South Wales Miners' Library in 1995. Mandy divides her working week between the South Wales Miners' Library and its branch library at the DOVE Workshop, Banwen.

TYRONE O'SULLIVAN was secretary of the Tower NUM Lodge for over twenty years, and attended the first NUM residential course at the South Wales Miners' Library in 1975. He was the Chair of Tower Colliery Ltd, the only workers' owned coal mine in the world.

DAI SMITH taught on the NUM courses at the South Wales Miners' Library in the 1970s and 1980s. He is co-author (with Hywel Francis) of *The Fed: A History of the South Wales Miners in the Twentieth Century* and many other books on Welsh cultural and social history, including the award winning *Raymond Williams: A Warrior's Tale*. He is currently Chair of the Arts Council of Wales, and holds the Raymond Williams Research Chair in Cultural History at Swansea University.

COLIN TROTMAN is Professor of Adult Continuing Education at Swansea University. He was one of the pioneers of Wales' first community based access to higher education programme and its educational guidance work. He is Vice-Chair of the Universities Association for Lifelong Learning in Wales. Prior to entering Swansea University, he worked as an electrician at Betws New Mine and Cwmgwili Colliery. He attended (and later organised) NUM courses at the South Wales Miners' Library.

SIÂN TUCKER is the Strategic Development Officer at the Black Mountain Centre, Brynaman. Prior to that, she worked as a Project Officer on the Community Archives Wales project, based at the South Wales Miners' Library.

CHRIS WILLIAMS is Professor of History and Head of the School of History, Archaeology and Religion at Cardiff University, and was previously Professor of Welsh History at Swansea University. He is a longstanding member of Llafur and researches and writes extensively on the history of the South Wales coalfield.

Index